THE SPARTANS

300 QUOTES, FACTS AND SAYINGS OF HISTORY'S GREATEST WARRIORS.

MICK KREMLING

Ó Copyright 2016 by Mick Kremling All rights reserved.

This document is geared towards providing exact and reliable information in regards to the topic and issue covered. The publication is sold with the idea that the publisher is not required to render accounting, officially permitted, or otherwise, qualified services. If advice is necessary, legal or professional, a practiced individual in the profession should be ordered.

From a Declaration of Principles which was accepted and approved equally by a Committee of the American Bar Association and a Committee of Publishers and Associations.

In no way is it legal to reproduce, duplicate, or transmit any part of this document in either electronic means or in printed format. Recording of this publication is strictly prohibited and any storage of this document is not allowed unless with written permission from the publisher. All rights reserved.

The information provided herein is stated to be truthful and consistent, in that any liability, in terms of inattention or otherwise, by any usage or abuse of any policies, processes, or directions contained within is the solitary and utter responsibility of the recipient reader. Under no circumstances will any legal responsibility or blame be held against the publisher for any reparation, damages, or monetary loss due to the information herein, either directly or indirectly.

Respective authors own all copyrights not held by the publisher.

The information herein is offered for informational purposes solely, and is universal as so. The presentation of the information is without contract or any type of guarantee assurance.

The trademarks that are used are without any consent, and the publication of the trademark is without permission or backing by the trademark owner. All trademarks and brands within this book are for clarifying purposes only and are the owned by the owners themselves, not affiliated with this document.

1

"SON, EITHER WITH THIS OR UPON THIS"

'REFERING TO HER SON'S SHIELD, A SPARTAN MOTHER

TO COME HOME WITHOUT HIS SHIELD WAS THE SIGN OF A DESERTER, THE COWARDLY WERE THOUGHT TO HAVE DISCARDED THEIR SHIELD WHILST THOSE WHO HAD DIED IN BATTLE WERE BROUGHT BACK UPON IT.

2

"SO THAT WE MAY GET CLOSE TO THE ENEMY"

AN UNNAMED SPARTAN, AFTER BEING ASKED WHY SPARTANS FOUGHT WITH SHORT SWORDS

3

A SPARTAN WARRIOR HAD PAINTED A LIFE SIZED DEPICTION OF A FLY UPON HIS SHIELD. WHEN ASKED WHY ANY ENEMY WOULD BE AFRAID OF A FLY, THE SPARTAN REPLIED:

"BECAUSE WHEN I SMASH IT INTO THE FOE'S FACE. IT WOULD APPEAR A GIANT"

(GREEKS WOULD OFTEN PAINT DEPICTIONS OF TERRIFYING CREATURES OR INTIMIDATING SYMBOLS ON THEIR SHIELDS, TO UNNERVE THE ENEMY.)

4

KING CLEOMENES, IN ANSWER TO THOSE OF THE ARGIVES WHO UPBRAIDED HIM AS AN IMPIOUS PERJURER, HE SAID,

"YOU HAVE THE POWER TO SPEAK ILL OF ME, BUT I HAVE THE POWER TO DO ILL TO YOU."

5

NEARING DEATH, KING AGESILAUS WAS APPROACHED AND ASKED IF A STATUE SHOULD ERECTED IN HIS HONOR. HE DECLINED, SAYING;

"IF I HAVE DONE ANYTHING NOBLE, THAT IS A SUFFICIENT MEMORIAL; IF I HAVE NOT, ALL THE STATUES IN THE WORLD WILL NOT PRESERVE MY MEMORY."

6

TO A MAN WHO WAS SURPRISED AT HOW SIMPLE KING AGESILAUS AND ALL SPARTANS' CLOTHS AND MEALS WERE, THE KING REPLIED:

"FREEDOM IS WHAT WE REAP FROM THIS WAY OF LIFE, MY FRIEND."

7

DEMARATUS, WHEN SOMEONE INQUIRED WHY HE WAS AN EXILE FROM SPARTA, BEING A KING, HE SAID:

"BECAUSE HER LAWS ARE MORE POWERFUL THAN I AM."

8

WHEN SOMEONE ELSE SAID, "THEY ARE NEAR TO US," HE SAID,

"GOOD, THEN WE ALSO ARE NEAR TO THEM."

-KING LEONIDAS

9

"NEITHER"

King Philip of Macedon, father of Alexander the Great, wrote a letter to the Spartans asking whether he should come to Sparta as a friend or as a foe; the Spartans returned the letter, replying with one word, "Neither". The Macedonian king took the advice and didn't go.

10

WHEN TOLD BY AN ATHENIAN THAT A MAN'S WORDS WERE THE MOST POWERFUL OF ALL,

THE SPARTAN KING AGIS' REPLIED:

"THEN WHEN YOU ARE SILENT, YOU ARE WORTHLESS."

11

"BEGIN WITH YOUR OWN FAMILY."

TO A MAN WHO ARGUED THAT SPARTA SHOULD SET UP A DEMOCRACY

LYCURGUS, THE LEGENDARY LAWMAKER OF SPARTA, REPLIED:

12

"COME AND TAKE THEM."

KING LEONIDAS' DEFIANT REPLY TO THE PERSIAN KING XERXES' COMMAND FOR THE SPARTANS TO LAY DOWN THEIR ARMS AT THE BATTLE OF THERMOPYLAE.

13

"BY NOT TRUSTING EVERYTHING TO FORTUNE."

-TO A MAN WHO ASKED A SPARTAN HOW HE MY BEST GAIN FAVOR WITH THE GODS AND LIVE A GOOD LIFE.

14

WHEN SOMEONE INQUIRED WHY THE SPARTANS HAD MADE TYRTAEUS THE POET A CITIZEN, HE SAID,

"SO A STRANGER SHALL NEVER APPEAR AS OUR LEADER."

15

WHEN A PERSIAN ASKED WHAT KIND OF GOVERNMENT HE COMMENDED MOST HIGHLY, HE SAID,

"THE GOVERNMENT WHICH DULY AWARDS WHAT IS FITTING TO BOTH THE BRAVE AND THE COWARDLY." LYSANDER OF SPARTA

16

THECTAMENES, WHEN THE EPHORS CONDEMNED HIM TO DEATH, WENT AWAY SMILING. SOMEONE AMONG THE BYSTANDERS ASKED HIM IF HE FELT SUCH CONTEMPT FOR THE LAWS OF SPARTA.

"NO," SAID HE, "BUT I REJOICE TO THINK THAT I MUST PAY THIS PENALTY MYSELF WITHOUT BEGGING OR BORROWING ANYTHING FROM ANYBODY."

17

IN A BATTLE HE WAS WOUNDED BY A SPEAR WHICH PIERCED HIS SHIELD, AND, PULLING THE WEAPON OUT OF THE WOUND, WITH THIS VERY SPEAR HE SLEW THE FOE. ASKED HOW HE GOT HIS WOUND, HE SAID,

"TWAS WHEN MY SHIELD TURNED TRAITOR."

18

ARCHIDAMUS, OBSERVING THAT HIS SON WAS FIGHTING IMPETUOUSLY AGAINST THE ATHENIANS, HE SAID,

"EITHER ADD TO YOUR STRENGTH, OR SUBTRACT FROM YOUR COURAGE."

19

PAEDARETUS, WHEN SOMEONE SAID THAT THE ENEMY WERE MANY IN NUMBER, REMARKED,

"THEN WE SHALL BE THE MORE FAMOUS, FOR WE SHALL KILL MORE MEN."

20

LEOTYCHIDAS, BEING ASKED WHAT FREEBORN BOYS HAD BEST LEARN, HE SAID,

"THOSE THINGS WHICH MAY HELP THEM WHEN THEY BECOME MEN."

21

"WHAT SPLENDID WOMEN'S QUARTERS."

WHILST BEING SHOWN TO A CITY'S SOLID –WALLS, WITH ITS REMARKABLE CRAFTSMANSHIP AND STRONG CONSTRUCTION, KING AGESILAUS REMARKED:

22

'STRANGER, IT WOULD BE MORE HONOURABLE FOR YOU TO BE CALLED A FRIEND OF YOUR OWN CITY'

KING THEOPOMPUS' REPLY, WHEN A FOREIGNER TOLD HIM THAT IN HIS OWN CITY, HE WAS CALLED A FRIEND OF SPARTA.

23

'SON, WITH EACH STEP YOU TAKE, BEAR COURAGE IN MIND.'

UNNAMED SPARTAN MOTHER, AS SHE WAS SENDING HER LAME SON UP THE BATTLEFIELD, SAID:

24

WHEN THE SPARTAN LYSANDER FINALLY ENTERED ATHENS TRIUMPHANTLY AND PUT AN END TO THE 27 YEAR PELOPONNESIAN WAR, HE SENT A MESSAGE BACK TO SPARTA THAT READ

"ATHENS IS TAKEN" THE REPLY BACK FROM THE EPHORS TO LYSANDER WAS "ALL YOU NEEDED TO SAY WAS 'TAKEN'.

25

"BY HERACLES! A MAN'S VALOR IS DEAD."

-ARCHIDAMUS SEEING A CATAPULT FIRE FOR THE FIRST TIME.

26

"MARRY A GOOD MAN, AND BARE GOOD CHILDREN."

-SPARTAN KING LEONIDAS TO HIS WIFE AS SHE ASKED HIM WHAT SHE SHOULD DO IF HE SHOULD NOT RETURN FROM THERMOPYLAE.

27

"THE SPARTANS ARE THE EQUAL OF ANY MEN WHEN THEY FIGHT AS INDIVIDUALS; FIGHTING TOGETHER AS A COLLECTIVE, THEY SURPASS ALL OTHER MEN."

-DAMARATUS TO XERXES.

28

WHEN PHILIP II'S ARMY WAS CONQUERING THE OTHER GREEK CITIES, HE WAS WEARY OF THE SPARTANS. ALTHOUGH THE SPARTAN'S AS A MILITARY POWER WERE NOW MUCH WEAKER THAN THE TIME OF THE PERSIAN WARS, PHILIP SENT THE SPARTANS A LETTER, HOPING TO REASON WITH THE SPARTANS AND AVOID THE POSSIBILITY OF HIS ARMY BEING DEFEATED BY A MUCH SMALLER FORCE. THE LETTER SENT READ:

"IF I ENTER LACONIA, I WILL BURN SPARTA TO THE GROUND."

THE REPLY FROM THE SPARTANS READ AS THIS:

"IF"

, NEITHER PHILIP NOR HIS SON ALEXANDER ATTEMPTED TO CAPTURE SPARTA.

29

"IT IS TRUE THAT THE ONES WHO COME OUT ON TOP ARE THE ONES WHO HAVE BEEN TRAINED IN THE HARDEST SCHOOL."

-KING ARCHIDAMUS II OF SPARTA

30

LYCURGUS WAS ASKED THE REASON FOR THE LESS THAN MODEST SACRIFICES SPARTA MADE TO THE GODS.

LYCURGUS REPLIED:

"SO THAT WE MAY ALWAYS HAVE SOMETHING TO OFFER."

31

"RISE UP SPARTANS, TAKE YOUR STAND AT ONE ANOTHER'S SIDES, FEET SET WIDE AND ROOTED AS OAKS IN THE GROUND."

-TYRTAEUS OF SPARTA

32

WHEN ASKED WHETHER JUSTICE OR BRAVERY WAS THE MOST IMPORTANT VIRTUE, AGESILAUS EXPLAINED,

"THERE IS NO USE FOR BRAVERY UNLESS JUSTICE IS PRESENT, AND NO NEED FOR BRAVERY IF ALL MEN ARE JUST."

33

RESPONDING TO A VISITOR WHO QUESTIONED WHY THEY PUT THEIR FIELDS IN THE HANDS OF THE **HELOTS** RATHER THAN CULTIVATE THEM THEMSELVES, ANAXANDRIDAS EXPLAINED,

"IT WAS BY CARING FOR THE FIELDS, BUT FOR OURSELVES, THAT WE ACQUIRED THOSE FIELDS."

34

WHEN AN ATHENIAN MAN ACCUSED THE SPARTANS OF BEING STUBBORN AND IGNORANT,

THE SPARTAN PLEISTOANAX AGREED, SAYING:

"WHAT YOU SAY IS TRUE. WE ALONE OF ALL THE GREEKS HAVE LEARNED NONE OF YOUR EVIL WAYS."

35

UPON BEING ASKED IF HE HAD HEARD THE MAN WHO COULD PERFECTLY IMITATE A NIGHTINGALE

A SPARTAN LAUGHED, SAYING:

"MY FRIEND, I HAVE HEARD THE NIGHTINGALE ITSELF."

36

AFTER AGESILAUS WAS WOUNDED IN ONE OF HIS MANY BATTLES AGAINST THEBES, ANTALCIDAS REMONSTRATED,

"THE THEBANS PAY YOU WELL FOR HAVING TAUGHT THEM TO FIGHT, WHICH THEY WERE NEITHER WILLING NOR ABLE TO DO BEFORE."

37

"IN WAR"

THE INSCRIPTION, ALONG WITH THE NAME OF THE SPARTAN, ENGRAVED ON HIS TOMBSTONE. SPARTAN MEN WOULD ONLY HAVE TOMBSTONES IF THEY DIED FIGHTING IN BATTLE. SPARTAN WOMEN RECEIVED THEM IF THEY DIED IN CHILDBIRTH.

38

"BECAUSE THE LATTER THEY PUT ON FOR THIER OWN PROTECTION, BUT THE SHIELD FOR THE COMMON GOOD OF THE WHOLE LINE."

-THE SPARTAN KING DEMARATOS EXPLAINING WHY IT WAS CONSIDERED A DISGRACE FOR A SPARTAN TO LOSE HIS SHIELD AND NOT HIS OTHER WEAPONS OR ARMOR.

39

"ADD A STEP FORWARD TO IT."

-SPARTAN MOTHER TO HER SON. THE SON WAS COMPLAINING HIS SWORD WAS TOO SHORT TO DO ANY GOOD.

40

"TELL THEM THAT THROUGHOUT THE ENTIRE TIME YOU SPOKE, I LISTENED"

WHEN A FOREIGN ENVOY ABRUPTLY STOPPED AFTER A LENGTHY SPEECH AND ASKED WHAT HE SHOULD TELL HIS MASTERS THE SPARTANS DECISION WAS,

KING AGIS' REPLIED:

41

AFTER HE WATCHED A SMALL BOY PULL A MOUSE OUT OF ITS BURROW, SEEING THE SMALL MOUSE TURN AROUND AND BITE THE BOY ON THE HAND AND ESCAPE, KING AGESILAUS WAS HEARD SAYING:.

'WHEN THE SMALLEST OF CREATURES DEFENDS ITSELF LIKE THIS, AGAINST AN ENEMY MUCH LARGER, TELL ME, WHAT OUGHT WE FREEMEN DO?'

42

WHEN ASKED BY A WOMAN FROM ATHENS: 'WHY ARE SPARTAN WOMEN THE ONLY ONES WHO CAN RULE MEN?' A SPARTAN WOMAN SAID:

'BECAUSE WE ARE THE ONLY ONES WHO GIVE BIRTH TO MEN.'

43

DAMONIDAS, BEING ASSIGNED TO THE LAST PLACE IN THE CHORUS BY THE DIRECTOR, EXCLAIMED,

"GOOD! YOU HAVE DISCOVERED, SIR, HOW THIS PLACE WHICH IS WITHOUT HONOUR MAY BE MADE A PLACE OF HONOUR."

44

THEARIDAS, AS HE WAS WHETTING HIS SWORD, WAS ASKED IF IT WAS SHARP, AND HE REPLIED,

"SHARPER THAN SLANDER."

45

IN ANSWER TO THE MAN WHO WAS WEAK IN BODY, BUT WAS URGING THAT THEY RISK A BATTLE AGAINST THE ENEMY BY BOTH LAND AND SEA, HE SAID,

"ARE YOU WILLING TO STRIP YOURSELF AND SHOW WHAT KIND OF MAN YOU ARE, YOU WHO ADVISE US TO FIGHT?"

-PAUSANIAS

46

IN ANSWER TO A MAN WHO RAISED THE QUESTION HOW ANYONE COULD POSSIBLY RULE IN SAFETY WITHOUT THE PROTECTION OF A BODYGUARD, HE SAID,

"IF ONE RULES HIS SUBJECTS AS FATHERS RULE THEIR SONS."

-KING AGASICLES

47

AN OLD MAN ATTENDING THE OLYMPIC GAMES COULD NOT FIND A SEAT TO WATCH. AS HE WENT FROM SEAT TO SEAT, HE WAS MET WITH INSULTS AND SCOLDINGS, NO MAN NOR BOY MADE ROOM FOR HIM. BUT WHEN HE CAME TO THE SPARTAN SECTION, ALL THE BOYS AND NEARLY ALL OF THE MEN QUICKLY STOOD UP AND OFFERED UP THEIR PLACE FOR THE OLD MAN TO SIT. WHEREUPON ALL THE OTHER GREEKS APPLAUDED, AND COMMENDED THE SPARTANS'

GENEROSITY BEYOND MEASURE; BUT THE OLD MAN, WITH TEARS IN HIS EYES, SAID:

"IT SEEMS ALL OF GREECE KNOWS WHAT THE RIGHT THING TO DO IS, BUT IT IS ONLY THE SPARTANS THAT DO IT."

48

"NOT HOW MANY BUT WHERE'"

AGIS II, 427 B.C.

THE SPARTANS USED TO ASK ABOUT THE ENEMY, IT WAS NOT IMPORTANT HOW MANY THERE ARE, BUT WHERE THE ENEMY WAS"

49

GO, TELL THE SPARTANS, STRANGER PASSING BY. THAT HERE, OBEDIENT TO THEIR LAWS, WE LIE.

-EPITAPH ON THE CENOTAPH OF THERMOPYLAE

50

"ARES IS LORD"

"GREECE HAS NO FEAR OF GOLD."

UPON BEING TOLD PERSIA HAD MORE GOLD THAN ANY OTHER NATION ON EARTH, THIS WAS THE REPLY.

51

"THESE ARE SPARTA'S WALLS."

WHEN ASKED WHY SPARTA HAD NO WALLS.

KING AGESILAUS' POINTED TO HIS MEN.

52

WHEN TOLD THAT 'SPARTA WAS PRESERVED BY HER KING'S MILITARY TALENT.,

KING THEOPOMPUS' REPLIED:

"NO, NOT BY HER KINGS, BUT BY HER CITIZEN'S READINESS TO OBEY."

53

"SO THAT OTHERS MAY NOT MAKE DECISIONS ON OUR BEHALF, BUT WE MAY FOR OTHERS."

UPON BEING ASKED WHY THE SPARTANS DRANK SO SPARINGLY, LEOTYCHIDAS REPLIED

54

PAEDARETUS, SEEING A CERTAIN MAN WHO WAS EFFEMINATE BY NATURE, BUT WAS COMMENDED BY THE CITIZENS FOR HIS MODERATION, HE SAID,

"PEOPLE SHOULD NOT PRAISE MEN WHO ARE LIKE TO WOMEN NOR WOMEN WHO ARE LIKE TO MEN, UNLESS SOME NECESSITY OVERTAKES THE WOMAN."

55

DEMARATUS, IN A COUNCIL MEETING HE WAS ASKED WHETHER IT WAS DUE TO FOOLISHNESS OR LACK OF WORDS THAT HE SAID NOTHING.

"BUT A FOOL," SAID HE, "WOULD NOT BE ABLE TO HOLD HIS TONGUE."

56

DAMIS, WITH REFERENCE TO THE INSTRUCTIONS SENT FROM ALEXANDER THAT THEY SHOULD PASS A FORMAL VOTE DEIFYING HIM, SAID,

"WE CONCEDE TO ALEXANDER THAT, IF HE SO WISHES, HE MAY BE CALLED A GOD."

57

BIAS, CAUGHT IN AN AMBUSH BY IPHICRATES THE ATHENIAN GENERAL, AND ASKED BY HIS SOLDIERS WHAT WAS TO BE DONE, SAID,

"WHAT ELSE EXCEPT FOR YOU TO SAVE YOUR LIVES AND FOR ME TO DIE FIGHTING?"

58

ARCHIDAMUS, IN ANSWER TO A MAN WHO PRAISED A HARPER AND EXPRESSED AMAZEMENT AT HIS ABILITY, HE SAID,

"MY GOOD SIR, WHAT HONOURS SHALL YOU BE ABLE TO OFFER TO GOOD MEN WHEN YOU HAVE SUCH PRAISE FOR A HARPER?"

59

WHEN LEO, THE SON OF EURYCRATIDAS, WAS ASKED WHAT KIND OF A CITY ONE COULD LIVE IN SO AS TO LIVE MOST SAFELY, HE SAID,

"WHERE THE INHABITANTS SHALL POSSESS NEITHER TOO MUCH NOR TOO LITTLE, AND WHERE RIGHT SHALL BE STRONG AND WRONG SHALL BE WEAK."

60

WHEN A PUBLIC LECTURER SPOKE AT CONSIDERABLE LENGTH ABOUT BRAVERY, HE BURST OUT LAUGHING AND WHEN THE MAN SAID, "WHY DO YOU LAUGH, CLEOMENES, AT HEARING A MAN SPEAK ABOUT BRAVERY, AND THAT, TOO, WHEN YOU ARE A KING?"

"BECAUSE, MY FRIEND," HE SAID, "IF IT HAD BEEN A SWALLOW SPEAKING ABOUT IT, I SHOULD HAVE DONE THE SAME THING, BUT IF IT HAD BEEN AN EAGLE, I SHOULD HAVE KEPT VERY QUIET."

61

HIPPOCRATIDAS, WHEN A YOUTH WITH A LOVER IN ATTENDANCE MET HIM ONE DAY, AND TURNED COLOUR, HE SAID:

"YOU OUGHT TO WALK WITH PERSONS SUCH THAT WHEN YOU ARE SEEN WITH THEM YOU SHALL KEEP THE SAME COMPLEXION."

62

"LET THE WEEPING BE FOR COWARDS: BUT YOU CHILD, I BURY WITHOUT A TEAR; YOU ARE MY SON, AND SPARTA'S TOO."

-WHEN A SPARTAN MOTHER HEARD THAT HER SON DIED IN THE BATTLE-LINE.

63

"IN SPARTA DWELL THOSE WHO ARE MOST ENSLAVED, YET THOSE WHO ARE MOST FREE."

-CRITIAS OF ATHENS

64

WHEN A MAN FROM ARGOS ACCUSED SPARTANS OF BEING SUSCEPTIBLE TO FOREIGN CORRUPTION,

EUDAMIDAS REPLIED:

"BUT YOU, WHEN YOU COME TO SPARTA, BECOME BETTER, NOT WORSE."

65

WHEN ASKED ON HOW THE SPARTANS MIGHT BEST PREVENT INVASION OF THEIR HOMELAND,

LYCURGUS ADVISED:

"BY REMAINING POOR AND FOR EACH CITIZEN DESIRING TO HAVE NO MORE THAN HIS FELLOW CITIZEN."

66

WHEN HE WAS ASKED WHY HE HAD COME TO FIGHT SUCH A HUGE ARMY WITH SO FEW MEN, KING LEONIDAS ANSWERED,

"IF NUMBERS WERE ALL THAT MATTERED, ALL THE MEN IN GREECE WOULD BE NO MATCH FOR EVEN HALF THE PERSIAN ARMY, BUT IF COURAGE IS WHAT MATTERS, I HAVE MORE THAN ENOUGH."

ON BEING AGAIN ASKED A SIMILAR QUESTION, HE REPLIED,

"I HAVE PLENTY, SINCE THEY ARE ALL TO BE SLAIN."

67

WHEN AN ATHENIAN CLAIMED THAT 'WE HAVE MANY A TIME DRIVEN YOU SPARTANS FROM THE CEPHISUS RIVER'.

ANTALCIDAS, A SPARTAN NEGOTIATOR'S REPLIED.

'BUT WE HAVE NEVER DRIVEN YOU FROM THE EUROTAS!'

'CEPHISUS' IS A RIVER THAT RUNS THROUGH THE ATHENIAN PLAIN, 'EUROTAS' IS A RIVER THAT FLOWS CLOSE TO SPARTA. NEVER HAD THE ATHENIANS, NOR ANY OTHER ENEMY, HAD EVER

REACHED THAT FAR IN SPARTAN TERRITORY.

68

"HOW GLORIOUS FALL THE VALIANT, SWORD IN HAND, IN BATTLE FOR THEIR NATIVE LAND."

-TYRTAEUS OF SPARTA

69

WHEN A RICH SUBORDINATE OF THE PERSIAN KING ASKED TWO SPARTANS WHY THEY WOULD NOT ALLY THEMSELVES WITH THE PERSIAN KING, WHO WAS RENOWNED FOR REWARDING HIS FRIENDS. FOR IF THEY, BEING MEN OF MERIT, WOULD ONLY SUBMIT TO HIM, HE WAS CERTAIN THE KING WOULD BESTOW UPON THEM ALL OF GREECE TO RULE AND GOVERN.

THIS WAS THEIR REPLY:

'THE SLAVE'S LIFE IS ALL YOU PERSIANS UNDERSTAND, YOU

KNOW NOTHING OF FREEDOM. FOR IF YOU DID, YOU WOULD HAVE ENCOURAGED US TO FIGHT ON, NOT JUST WITH OUR SWORD AND SPEAR, BUT WITH TOOTH AND NAIL, NAY, EVERYTHING WE POSSESS.'

70

POLYCRATIDAS, A SPARTAN SENT ON A DIPLOMATIC MISSION TO A PERSIAN GENERAL, WAS ASKED WHETHER THEY CAME IN A PRIVATE OR A PUBLIC CAPACITY, THE SPARTAN ANSWERED,

"IF WE SUCCEED, PUBLIC;

IF NOT, PRIVATE.

71

"OUR TRACHINIAN FRIEND BRINGS US JOYOUS NEWS. FOR IF THE MEDES INTEND TO BLOT OUT THE SUN, WE SHALL HAVE OUR FIGHT IN THE SHADE!"

A SPARTAN, ANSWERING THE TERRIFIED TRACHINIAN, SAID, 'SUCH IS THE BARBARIAN'S NUMBERS THAT THEIR ARROWS, UPON BEING LOOSED, WOULD BLOT OUT THE SUN.'

72

WHEN A FELLOW SPARTAN ARGUED IN FAVOR OF WAR WITH MACEDON CITING THEIR VICTORIES OVER THE PERSIANS,

KING EUDAMIDAS RETORTED

"YOU SEEM NOT TO REALIZE THAT YOUR PROPOSAL IS THE SAME AS FIGHTING FIFTY WOLVES AFTER DEFEATING A THOUSAND SHEEP."

73

"FEAR MAKES MEN DO THEIR BEST TO TAKE SHELTER BEHIND THE SHIELD OF THE MAN TO HIS RIGHT. THINKING THE CLOSER THEY ARE TOGETHER, THE SAFER THEY WILL BE."

-THUCYDIDES DESCRIBING WHY HOPLITE BATTLES ALWAYS EDGED TOWARDS THE RIGHT

74

WHEN HER SON APPROACHED HER, SHE ASKED HIM 'HOW FAIRED THE WAR?' HER SON REPLIED, 'ALL THE MEN WERE DEAD', SHE THEN, WITHOUT A SECOND THOUGHT, PICKED UP A KNIFE AND KILLED HIM SAYING...

"DID YOU EXPECT ME TO BELIEVE YOU WERE SENT BACK TO BRING YOUR MOTHER THE BAD NEWS?

-A SPARTAN MOTHER, REALIZING HER SON'S COWARDICE

75

KING CLEOMENES, WHEN THE PEOPLE OF ARGOS ASSERTED THAT THEY WOULD WIPE OUT THEIR FORMER DEFEAT BY FIGHTING AGAIN, HE SAID,

"I WONDER IF BY THE ADDITION OF A WORD OF TWO SYLLABLES YOU HAVE NOW BECOME MORE POWERFUL THAN YOU WERE BEFORE!

76

PLEISTOANAX, THE SON OF PAUSANIAS, WHEN AN ATTIC ORATOR CALLED THE SPARTANS UNLEARNED, SAID,

"YOU ARE QUITE RIGHT, FOR WE ALONE OF THE GREEKS HAVE LEARNED NO EVIL FROM YOU."

77

WHEN ONE OF THE HELOTS CONDUCTED HIMSELF RATHER BOLDLY TOWARD HIM, HE SAID,

"IF I WERE NOT ANGRY, I WOULD KILL YOU."

-CHARILLUS OF SPARTA

78

IN ANSWER TO A MAN WHO SAID THAT HE COMMENDED HIM AND WAS VERY FOND OF HIM, HE SAID

"I HAVE TWO OXEN IN A FIELD, AND ALTHOUGH THEY BOTH MAY UTTER NO SOUND, I KNOW PERFECTLY WELL WHICH ONE IS LAZY AND WHICH ONE IS THE WORKER."

-LYSANDER OF SPARTA

79

"HAVE A GOOD BREAKFAST MEN, FOR TONIGHT WE DINE IN HADES!"

KING LEONIDAS' FAMOUS WORDS TO HIS MEN AT THERMOPYLAE. HE BID THEM ENJOY THEIR BREAKFAST AS NOBODY THOUGHT THAT THEY WOULD SURVIVE THE DAY;

THEY DIDN'T.

80

"PAEDARETUS, UPON HEARING HE WOULD NOT BE ONE OF THE 300 SELECTED TO ACCOMPANY LEONIDAS AT THERMOPYLAE, WAS SAID TO HAVE BEEN CHEERFUL. SMILING, WAS SAID TO BE GLAD THAT SPARTA POSSESSED 300 CITIZENS WHO WHERE BETTER THAN HIM."

-PLUTARCH, SAYINGS OF KINGS AND COMMANDERS

81

KING LEONIDAS, BEING ASKED WHY THE BEST OF MEN PREFER A GLORIOUS DEATH TO AN INGLORIOUS LIFE, HE SAID,

"BECAUSE THEY BELIEVE THE ONE TO BE NATURE'S GIFT BUT THE OTHER TO BE WITHIN THEIR OWN CONTROL."

82

BEING ASKED WHY THE SPARTANS RISKED THEIR LIVES SO BRAVELY IN WAR, HE SAID,

"BECAUSE THEY HAVE LEARNED TO RESPECT THEIR COMMANDERS AND NOT TO FEAR THEM."

-POLYDORUS

83

WHEN A SPARTAN BOY REACHED THE AGE OF SEVEN, IT WAS TAKEN FROM HIS MOTHER AND GIVEN TO THE STATE. A RIGOROUS DISCIPLINE AND MAINLY MILITARY TYPE EDUCATION, THE SO-CALLED AGOGE, COMMENCED, LASTING TWELVE YEARS. AT THE AGE OF TWENTY, WHEN THE AGOGE ENDED, THE MILITARY SERVICE OF THE SPARTAN BEGUN.

84

SPARTAN WOMEN WERE RESPECTED, WELL-EDUCATED AND HAD MORE STATUS AND POWER THAN WOMEN LIVING IN THE OTHER GREEK CITY-STATES.

85

SPARTAN BABIES WERE SOMETIMES BATHED IN WINE INSTEAD OF WATER. BABIES WERE NOT PICKED UP WHEN THEY CRIED VERY OFTEN IN AN EFFORT TO MAKE THEM TOUGH.

86

SPARTAN MEN WERE SOLDIERS UNTIL THEY WERE 60 YEARS OLD. IN TIMES OF DIRE NEED, ALL MEN, REGARDLESS OF AGE, COULD BE CALLED UPON TO SERVE IN BATTLE.

87

AS FOR PROPER EDUCATION, THEY WERE TAUGHT ONLY THE BASICS OF HOW TO READ AND WRITE AND TO WASTE NO WORDS SPEAKING TO THE POINT (LACONIZEIN). THEY ALSO LEARNED MILITARY POEMS, WAR SONGS, HOW TO DANCE AND RECITED HOMER.

88

SPARTIATES WERE THE ÉLITE OF SPARTAN SOCIETY. THEY WERE ENTITLED TO ALL THE POLITICAL AND LEGAL RIGHTS THE STATE OFFERED. TO JOIN THE SPARTIATES, YOU HAD TO BE A 'HIGH-BORN' MAN WHO HAD COMPLETED HIS MILITARY TRAINING. THE SPARTIATES WERE VERY FEW. IT HAS BEEN ESTIMATED THAT OF A POPULATION OF NEARLY 200,000, PERHAPS FEWER THAN 8,000 WERE FULL SPARTAN CITIZENS.

89

SPARTIATES AND OTHER SPARTAN CITIZENS WERE NOT PERMITTED TO ENTER ANY PROFESSION EXCEPT THE MILITARY.

90

ALL THE KINGS OF SPARTA WERE SAID TO BE DESCENDANTS OF THE GREEK HERO OF LEGEND, HERACLES.

91

THE SPARTANS CONSIDERED FOOTWEAR FOR SOLDIERS TO MAKE THE MEN 'SOFT'. WHEN A SPARTAN YOUTH TRAINED, HE WAS BAREFOOT BECAUSE IT WAS BELIEVED HE WOULD BE MORE HARDENED FOR BATTLE IF HE DID NOT KNOW THE COMFORT OF SOFT LEATHER ON HIS FEET.

92

IN PREPARATION FOR MARRIAGE, SPARTAN WOMEN WOULD HAVE THEIR HEADS SHAVED; AFTER THEY WED, THEIR HAIR WAS KEPT SHORT.

93

FOR A LONG TIME THE SPARTANS HAD NO CITY WALLS, TRUSTING TO THE STRENGTH OF THEIR ARMY FOR DEFENSE AGAINST INVADERS AND AGAINST THEIR OWN LACONIAN AND MESSENIAN SUBJECTS.

94

IF A SPARTAN CITIZEN WERE ACCUSED OF COWARDICE, GOVERNMENT RULINGS COULD BE INVOLVED THAT COULD EXCLUDE HIM FROM HOLDING ANY OFFICE IN SPARTA. IF COWARDICE WAS PROVEN, THE CITIZEN WOULD BE BANNED FROM MAKING ANY LEGAL CONTRACT OR AGREEMENT, INCLUDING MARRIAGE.

95

DURING THE AGOGE, BOYS SLEPT ON RUSHES THAT THEY GATHERED FROM THE RIVER BANK THEMSELVES. IF THEY WERE COLD IN WINTER THEN THEY MIXED A FEW THISTLES IN WITH THE REEDS ... THE PRICKLING GAVE THEM A FEELING OF WARMTH.

96

SPARTAN KINGS WERE ACCOMPANIED BY HANDPICKED GROUP OF 300 MEN WHO SERVED AS A ROYAL GUARD

97

THOUGH AT TIMES THE FIERCEST OF ENEMIES, MANY OF THE NOBLEST AND BEST OF ATHENIAN SOCIETY ALWAYS ADMIRED, AND CONSIDERED SPARTAN WAY OF LIFE AS AN IDEAL THEORY REALIZED IN PRACTICE.

98

TO PREPARE SPARTANS FOR THE HARSHENESS OF WAR AND INSTILL DISCIPLINE, SPARTANS WERE ALWAYS SERVED BLAND FOOD IN MESS HALLS AND IN LESS THAN FILLING QUANTITIES.

99

THE SPARTANS WOULD DECLARE WAR ON THEIR ENTIRE HELOT SLAVE POPULATION EACH YEAR TO INSTILL FEAR AND KEEP THEM SUBJUGATED.

100

SPARTA WOULD GROW IN POPULATION UP UNTIL THE FIRST MESSENIAN WAR IN 736 BC. THEY WOULD GO ON TO DEFEAT THE MESSENIANS AND ENSLAVE THE ENTIRE POPULATION. THEY WOULD BECOME KNOWN AS THE HELOTS.

101

SPARTA WAS THE FIRST GREEK CITY- TO DEVELOP A COMPLEX SYSTEM OF MUTUAL DEFENSIVE TREATIES.

SPARTA REPEATEDLY INTERVENED TO DEFEND DEMOCRACY AGAINST TYRANNY. SPARTAN DIPLOMACY WAS ARGUABLY MORE EFFECTIVE THAN SPARTAN MILITARY MIGHT IN MAINTAINING SPARTA'S RENOWNED STATUS FOR CENTURIES.

102

WHEN SOMEONE INQUIRED HOW MUCH PROPERTY TELECUS POSSESSED, HE SAID,

"NOT MORE THAN ENOUGH."

103

THE SPARTANS, DESPITE SPECULATION, WERE LITERATE AND WERE KNOWN FOR THE SHARP INTELLECT AND VERBAL SKILLS.

SOCRATES HIMSELF SAYS

"THE MOST ANCIENT HOMES OF PHILOSOPHY IN GREECE ARE CRETE AND SPARTA, WHERE MORE SOPHISTS ARE TO BE FOUND THAN ANYWHERE ELSE."

104

THE SPARTANS VIEWED MARRIAGE PRIMARILY AS A MEANS TO PRODUCE MORE FIGHTING MEN, FOR SPARTA. A WOMAN WAS EXPECTED TO TAKE INTO CONSIDERATION THE HEALTH AND ATHLETICISM OF HER FUTURE HUSBAND.

105

SPARTAN BACHELORS WERE MOCKED AND REDICULED AT PUBLIC EVENTS OR FESTIVALS, SEEN AS HAVING NEGLECTED THEIR DUTY TO SPARTA.

106

ALTHOUGH WINE WAS A STAPLE OF THEIR DIET, SPARTANS WOULD RARELY DRINK TO INTOXICATION. FROM EARLY ON, SPARTAN CHILDREN WERE WARNED AGAINST THE WEAKNESS AND VULNERABILITY OF DRUNKENESS.

107

THE SPARTAN KING, AGIS WAS DEFEATED BY A MACEDONIAN ARMY. THE KING, UNABLE TO WALK AND DYING FROM HIS WOUNDS, ORDERED THE REST OF THE SPARTAN ARMY TO WITHDRAW. KING AGIS, BARELY ABLE TO STAND, SLEW HALF A DOZEN MACEDONIAN SOLDIERS BEFORE BEING KILLED BY A JAVELIN.

108

THE SPARTANS CARRIED A SHORT SWORD CALL THE XIPHOS. THE XIPHOS WAS TYPICALLY ABOUT 2 FEET LONG, THOUGH THE SPARTAN'S VERSION WAS ONLY ABOUT A FOOT LONG. THE SWORD ITSELF WAS USED IN A STABBING MOTION, IN BATTLE WHERE QUARTERS WERE TOO CLOSE TO WIELD A SPEAR EFFECTIVELY SPARTANS WERE TRAINED ALL THEIR LIFE TO INDENTIFY THE WEAK POINTS IN ENEMY ARMOR AND WERE EXTREMELY DEADLY WITH THE BLADE.

109

"IT WAS COMMON PERCEPTION THAT SPARTANS WOULD NEVER LAY DOWN THEIR ARMS FOR ANY REASON, BE IT DANGER, HUNGER, OR EXHAUSTION."

-THUCYDIDES

110

DURING A CAMPAIGN, SPARTAN KINGS AND OFFICERS WOULD OFFER SACRIFICE EACH MORNING AND ON THE EVE OF A BATTLE. IF THE OMENS WERE ILL, HE MAY DECIDE TO NOT ENGAGE THE ENEMY OR NOT MARCH.

111

SOMEONE ASKED, "AFTER YOUR FREQUENT WARS WITH THE ARGIVES, WHY HAVE YOU NOT WIPED THEM OUT?" THE SPARTAN REPLIED,

"WE WOULDN'T WISH TO WIPE THEM OUT BECAUSE WE NEED SPARING PARTNERS FOR OUR YOUNG MEN."

112

"THE SPARTANS FOUGHT IN A WAY WORTHY OF NOTE, AND SHOWED THEMSELVES FAR MORE SKILLFUL IN BATTLE THAN THE BARBARIANS, OFTEN TURNING ABOUT AND ACTING AS IF TO RETREAT. THE PERSIANS WOULD RUSH AFTER THEM SHOUTING, THE SPARTANS WOULD THEN TURN ROUND AND FACE THE ENEMY, IN THIS WAY THEY CAUSE SEVERE CASUALITIES AMONG THE ENEMY."

-HERODOTUS

113

THE SYSSITIA WAS MADE UP OF 15 OTHERS AND THE SOLDIER WOULD EAT AND SLEEP WITH HIS SYSSITIA UNTIL THE AGE OF 30

114

KING LEONIDAS KNEW THE DEFENSE OF THERMOPYLAE, WITH ONLY 300 SPARTANS AND 6,000 GREEKS, AGAINST A HUGE PERSIAN ARMY WOULD BE A SUICIDE MISSION, AND THUS ONLY SELECTED MEN WITH CHILDREN TO CARRY ON THEIR FAMILY LINES.

115

THE SPARTANS FOUGHT IN THE PHALANX FORMATION. THE PHALANX IS A RECTANGULAR MILITARY FORMATION, USUALLY COMPOSED ENTIRELY OF HEAVY INFANTRY ARMED WITH SPEARS OR PIKES DEPENDING ON THE ARMY'S CHOICE OF WEAPONRY.

116

THE LACONIC PHRASE IMPLIES A CONCISE STATEMENT THAT STILL MANAGES TO DRIVE HOME ITS POINT; AND AS SUCH THE SCOPE ENTAILS THE USE OF VERY FEW WORDS (BY A PERSON OR SPEECH). THIS TERM ITSELF COMES FROM THE GEOGRAPHICAL REGION OF LACONIA, WHICH COMPRISED OF THE CITY STATE OF SPARTA

117

SPARTANS WERE ALLOWED TO KILL HELOTS IF THEY BE TOO CHARISMATIC, SMART, OR FIT, AMONG OTHER REASONS.

118

SPARTANS, FOR ONE OF MANY REASONS, WORE THEIR HAIR LONG. REASON BEING THAT LONG HAIR HAD ALWAYS BEEN ASSOCIATED WITH FREEDOM IN ARCHAIC SPARTAN CIRCLES, SINCE MANY LOWLY SERVILE TASKS COULD NOT BE DONE WITH LONG HAIR.

119

WOMEN DID NOT FIGHT IN THE ARMY BUT WERE REQUIRED TO PARTICIPATE IN PHYSICAL ACTIVITY TO ENSURE GOOD HEALTH AND STRONG BABIES.

120

ALL ADULT MEN BELONGED TO 'MESSES'- SMALL GROUPS THAT MET AND DINED TOGETHER AND WERE HOUSED IN INDIVIDUAL 'MEN'S HOUSES'.

121

SPARTAN BOYS WERE TAKEN TO THE SANCTUARY OF ARTEMIS ORTHIA TO BE FLOGGED TO SHOW THEIR TOUGHNESS AND ENDURANCE. IT WAS NOT UNCOMMON FOR SOME BOYS TO DIE DURING THE FLOGGING RATHER THAN SHOW WEAKNESS OR PAIN.

122

TWO KINGS RULED SPARTA AT ALL TIMES. ONE WAS TO COME FROM THE AGIAD FAMILY AND THE OTHER FROM THE EURYPONTID FAMILY.

123

THE INHABITANTS OF SPARTA WERE DIVIDED INTO DIFFERENT SOCIAL GROUPS.

SPARTIATES WERE THE FULL CITIZENS WHO ENJOYED ALL RIGHTS. **MOTHAKES** WERE THE NON-SPARTAN BORN FREE MEN WHO WORKED AS ARTISANS OR IN SKILLED TRADES. **PERIOKOI** WERE SLAVES WHO HAD BEEN FREED BY THEIR SPARTAN MASTERS. **HELOTS**, THE LOWEST IN THE SYSTEM, WERE THE SLAVES TAKEN FROM MESSENIA.

124

HEARING A PHILOSOPHER DISCOURSING TO THE EFFECT THAT THE WISE MAN IS THE ONLY GOOD GENERAL, A SPARTAN SAID,

"THE SPEECH IS ADMIRABLE, BUT THE SPEAKER IS NOT TO BE TRUSTED; FOR HE HAS NEVER BEEN AMID THE BLARE OF TRUMPETS."

125

"HERE IS COURAGE, MANKIND'S FINEST POSSESSION, HERE IS THE NOBLEST PRIZE THAT A YOUNG MAN CAN ENDEAVOR TO WIN"

-TYRTAEUS OF SPARTA

126

DURING THE OLYMPIC GAMES A SPARTAN WAS OFFERED A FORTUNE IN BRIBES TO THROW A WRESTLING MATCH. HE REFUSED. AFTER A GRUELING MATCH, THE SPARTAN BEAT HIS OPPONENT.

ANGRY, THE BRIBESTER ASKED HIM "WHAT HAVE YOU GAINED BY YOUR VICTORY SPARTAN?"

THE SPARTAN REPLIED WITH A SMILE

"IN BATTLE, PRIDE OF PLACE, IN FRONT OF THE KING."

127

A SPARTAN WAS TAUGHT THAT LOYALTY TO THE STATE CAME BEFORE EVERYTHING ELSE IN LIFE, INCLUDING ONE'S FAMILY.

128

IN 432 BC, AN ASSEMBLY FROM ALL THE GREEK CITIES, TROUBLED BY THE GROWING INFLUENCE OF ATHENS, GATHERED AT SPARTA. A DELEGATION FROM ATHENS WAS ALSO PRESENT. MANY GREEK CITIES WARNED THAT IF THE SPARTANS REMAINED PASSIVE, THEY WOULD LOSE THEIR ALLIES AND MILITARY STATUS AMONG THEIR FELLOW GREEKS AND ATHENS WOULD BECOME THE SOLE DOMINANT POWER IN HELLAS (GREECE). AFTER MUCH DEBATE, THE MAJORITY OF THE

SPARTAN ASSEMBLY VOTED IN FAVOR FOR WAR AGAINST ATHENS, THUS EFFECTIVELY BEGINNING THE PELOPONESIAN WAR.

129

SOMEONE ON SEEING A PAINTING IN WHICH SPARTANS WERE DEPICTED AS SLAIN BY ATHENIANS, KEPT REPEATING, "BRAVE, BRAVE ATHENIANS."

A SPARTAN CUT IN WITH,

"YES, IN THE PICTURE AT LEAST!"

130

SOME PEOPLE, ENCOUNTERING SPARTANS ON THE ROAD, SAID, "YOU ARE IN LUCK, FOR ROBBERS HAVE JUST LEFT THIS PLACE," BUT THEY SAID, "EGAD, NO, BUT IT IS THEY WHO ARE IN LUCK FOR NOT ENCOUNTERING US."

131

THE SPARTANS ABHORRED THE USE BOWS AND ARCHERY AS A SKILL. PLUTARCH RELATES TO HOW A SPARTAN WARRIOR WAS MORTALLY WOUNDED BY AN ENEMY ARCHER. WHILE LYING ON THE GROUND, HE WAS NOT WORRIED ABOUT HIS DEATH, BUT RATHER REMORSEFUL THAT HE WOULD DIE AT THE HAND OF A 'WOMANISH' ARCHER.

132

ABSTINENCE OF PLEASURE AND SELF-DISCIPLINE, NOT MINDLESS OBIDIENCE WAS THE MAIN GOAL OF THE SPARTAN EDUCATION SYSTEM. THE SPARTANS PLACED EQUALITY (FOR CITIZENS), LIBERTY, AND BROTHERHOOD AT THE CORE OF THEIR ETHICAL SYSTEM.

133

"DIG IT OUT YOURSELF."

KING LEONIDAS KICKED A PERSIAN MESSENGER THAT CAME TO SPARTA TO ASK FOR THEIR SURRENDER DOWN A WELL. IT'S RECORDED, HOWEVER, THAT THE ACTUAL QUOTE AS HE DID THIS WAS: 'DIG IT OUT FOR YOURSELVES' IN RELATION TO THE REQUIRED SURRENDER PAYMENT OF EARTH AND WATER.

134

GREEK PHILOSOPHERS, ESPECIALLY PLATONISTS, WOULD DESCRIBE SPARTA AS THE IDEAL CULTURE. THE SPARTANS WERE STRONG, BRAVE, AND FREE FROM CORRUPTION OF MONEY AND COMMERCE.

135

IT WAS CUSTOM FOR SPARTANS TO WASH AND DRESS THEIR HAIR WHEN THEY INTENDED TO PUT THEIR LIVES IN GREAT DANGER.

136

ON THE 5TH DAY, XERXES SENT IN THE MEDES AND CISSIANS, WITH ORDERS TO TAKE THE SPARTANS ALIVE AND BRING THEM TO HIM. THE MEDES CHARGES FORWARD IN VAST NUMBERS AND WOULD NOT WITHDRAW THOUGH THEY SUFFERED HORRENDOUS LOSSES.

-BATTLE OF THERMOPYLAE

137

ATHENS AND SPARTA FOUNDED THE "HELLENIC LEAGUE", A UNITED COALITION OF GREEK CITIES TO COMBAT THE ENORMOUS PERSIAN INVASION.

138

SPARTA WAS THE ONLY GREEK CITY TO INTRODUCE LAND REFORM AIMED AT EQUALIZING WEALTH AMONG HER CITIZENS.

139

SPARTAN WOMEN TOOK PRIDE IN THEIR INTELLECTUAL ACCOMPLISHMENTS AND ECONOMIC POWER. THEY WERE NOT AFRAID TO EXPRESS THEIR OPINIONS AND SPEAK BLATENTLY IN THE PRESENCE OF MEN,– LEADING OTHER GREEKS TO CONDEMN THEM AS UNDISCIPLINED, IMMORAL, AND DANGEROUS.

140

"AS FAR AS THIS CAN REACH."

WHEN ASKED BY A FOREIGNER 'HOW FAR SPARTA'S DOMAIN STRETCHED?' KING AGESILAUS' REPLIED BY LEVELING HIS SPEAR.

141

IN HOMER'S THE ILIAD, MENELAUS, KING OF SPARTA, CHALLENGED PARIS, THE PRINCE OF TROY, TO A DUEL FOR HELEN'S RETURN. MENELAUS, BEFORE HE CAN KILL PARIS AND RECLAIM HIS WIFE, IS DENIED HIS VICTORY BY THE GODDESS APHRODITE SPRIRITS THE PRINCE AWAY TO THE WALLS OF TROY.

142

"THE BATTLE OF CHAMPIONS",

IT WAS A BATTLE THAT TOOK PLACE BETWEEN SPARTA AND ARGOS. EACH CITY HANDPICKED 300 WARRIORS TO SEND TO THE BATTLE. THE FIGHTING THAT ENSUED WAS SO FIERCE, THAT AT THE END, THE ONLY ONES LEFT WERE TWO EXHAUSTED ARGIVES AND ONE WOUNDED SPARTAN. THE MEN FROM ARGOS RETURNED HOME, WHILE THE SPARTAN KILLED HIMSELF IN SHAME. BOTH CITIES WOULD CLAIM VICTORY. THE SPARTANS CLAIMING THE ARGIVES FLED THE FIELD, AND

THE ARGIVES CLAIMING ALL THE SPARTAN SOLDIERS HAD DIED. THE TWO CITIES WOULD BECOME BITTER RIVALS.

143

THE SPARTAN WAY OF LIFE WAS ENTIRELY DEPENDENT ON THE SYSTEMATIC OPPRESION AND EXPLOITATION OF THEIR HELOT SLAVES. EACH INDIVIDUAL SPARTAN AT WAR WAS SAID TO BE ATTENEDED BY UP TO SEVEN HELOT SERVANTS.

144

HISTORIANS DATE THE ORIGIN OF THE HOPLITE PHALANX TO THE 8TH CENTURY BC IN SPARTA,

145

A SPARTAN PHALANX, ALONG WITH MOST OTHER GREEKS, USUALLY DEPLOYED IN RANKS OF 8 MEN OR MORE DEEP.

146

DESPITE ITS UNSTOPPABLE FORWARD MOMENTUM, A PHALANX WAS VERY SUSCEPTIBLE TO A MORE MOBILE, FLEXIBLE OPPONENT THAT COULD OUT FLANK THE PHALANX.

147

EACH HOPLITE IN PHALANX FORMATION WOULD CARRY HIS SHIELD ON THE LEFT ARM, PROTECTING NOT ONLY HIMSELF BUT HIS COMRADE ON HIS LEFT.

148

A PHALANX FORMATION WAS ONLY AS STRONG AS ITS WEAKEST LINK. IF ANY INDIVIDUAL MAN BROKE RANK, THE ENTIRE COHESION IF THE FORMATION WAS AT RISKED OF COLLAPSED.

149

SPARTANS WERE EVER READY FOR CONFLICT. A SPARTAN WAS CONTINUOUSLY TAUGHT NEVER TO LEAVE HIS WEAPON OUTSIDE ARM'S REACH WHETHER ON CAMPAIGN OR AT HOME IN SPARTA.

150

"SUCH SERIOUSNESS THE BOYS MADE OF THE MATTER OF STEALING, THAT WHEN ONE OF THEM WAS CAUGHT CARRYING UNDER HIS TUNIC A STOLEN YOUNG FOX, THE BOY REMAINED SILENT WHILST THE ANIMAL PROCEEDED TO CLAW AND TEAR OUT HIS BOWELS WITH IT'S TEETH AND CLAWS, AND DIED RATHER THAN REVEAL HIS THEFT."

-PLUTARCH, ON A SPARTAN YOUTH DURING THE AGOGE

151

FULL CITIZENS, KNOWN AS THE SPARTIATES, OR HÓMOIOI ("EQUALS") RECEIVED A GRANT OF LAND FOR THEIR MILITARY SERVICE.

152

"...LEARN TO LOVE DEATH'S INK-BLACK SHADOW AS MUCH AS YOU LOVE THE LIGHT OF DAWN."

-TYRTAEUS OF SPARTA

153

SUICIDAL RECKLESSNESS AND RAGE WERE STRICTLY FORBIDDON IN THE ARMY. THESE KINDS OF BEHAVIORS WERE SEEN AS ENDANGERING YOUR FELLOW SOLDIERS AND THE COHESION OF THE PHALANX AS A WHOLE.

154

THE SPARTAN SLAVES, THE HELOTS, ARE UNIQUE IN THE HISTOY OF SLAVES. UNLIKE OTHER SLAVES, HELOTS HAD A GOOD AMOUNT OF PRIVILIGES SUCH AS BEING ALLOWED TO EARN AND KEEP WEALTH. SOME HELOTS ARE KNOWN TO HAVE EVEN BOUGHT THEIR FREEDOM FROM THE STATE,

155

THE SPARTANS LEFT BEHIND LITTLE ARCHITECTUAL WONDERS AND IF A PERSON WAS TO TRAVEL TO THE ANCIENT RUINS OF SPARTA, HE WOULD FIND IT HARD TO BELIEVE SUCH A PEOPLE HAD LIVED THEIR AT ALL, SO LITTLE PHYSICAL EVIDENCE REMAINS.

156

INITIALLY SPARTA WAS VERY HESITANT TO BEGIN A CONFLICT WITH PERSIA. THE PERSIAN KING WAS THREATENING THE GREEK CITIES ON THE IONIAN COAST (MODERN TURKEY). THE GREEKS WHO LIVED THERE, SENT AN EMISSARY TO SPARTA TO PLEAD FOR AID. THE SPARTANS REFUSED BUT THREATENED THE PERSIAN KING CYRUS, TELLING HIM TO HALT ANY AGGRESSION AGAINST THE GREEK CITIES. "HE WAS TO HARM NO GREEK CITY, REGARDLESS OF LOCATION, ELSE

THE SPARTANS MOBILIZE FOR WAR,"

-HERODOTUS

157

IF ACCOUNTS OF COWARDICE PROVEN, THE PERSON WAS MADE TO WEAR SPECIALLY DESIGNED CLOAKS WITH MULTIFARIOUS COLORS AND ALSO HAD TO SHAVE HALF THEIR BEARD. SUCH KINDS OF BITTER EPISODES FREQUENTLY LED TO SUICIDES AMONG THE SPARTAN MEN WHO SURRENDERED IN BATTLES

158

A SPARTAN, PASSING BY A TOMB AT NIGHT, AND IMAGINING THAT HE SAW A GHOST, RAN AT IT WITH UPLIFTED SPEAR, AND, AS HE THRUST AT IT, HE EXCLAIMED,

"WHERE ARE YOU FLEEING FROM ME, YOU SOUL THAT SHALL DIE TWICE?"

159

A SPARTAN WHO HAD SORE TROUBLE WITH HIS EYES WAS GOING FORTH TO WAR; AND WHEN SOME SAID TO HIM, "WHERE ARE YOU GOING IN THAT STATE, OR WHAT DO YOU PROPOSE TO DO?"

HE SAID,

"EVEN IF I ACCOMPLISH NOTHING ELSE, I MAY AT LEAST BLUNT AN ENEMY'S SWORD."

160

WHEN TWO BROTHERS QUARRELLED WITH EACH OTHER, THE SPARTANS FINED THE FATHER BECAUSE HE PERMITTED HIS SONS TO QUARREL.

161

TO A MAN WHO WAS BEING PUNISHED, AND KEPT SAYING, "I DID WRONG UNWILLINGLY,"

SOMEONE RETORTED,

"THEN TAKE YOUR PUNISHMENT UNWILLINGLY."

162

NOT ONLY WERE THE SPARTANS SUPERB ON THE BATTLEFIELD AS WARRIORS, THEY WERE ALSO EXPERT TACTICIANS. THEIR WELL DESERVED REPUTATION AS FEARLESS, EFFICIENT, DISCIPINED SOLDIERS WAS WIDESPREAD. THEY WERE ALSO EXCELLENT PEACEMAKERS AND ALLIES. THE SPARTANS WERE INVOLVED IN COUNTLESS BATTLES AMONG THE GREEK CITY-STATES AND FEARED BY ALL.

163

BEGINNING IN 743 BC AND SPANNING THE NEXT TWENTY YEARS, THE FIRST MESSIANIC WAR WAS A CONFLICT THE SPARTANS EVENTUALLY WON. THE WAR WAS THOUGHT TO HAVE BEGUN OVER SPARTA'S DESIRE FOR THE RICH MESSENIAN LANDS.

164

BEFORE 500 BC, SPARTA HAD FORMED A CONFEDERACY OF ALLIES (THE PELOPONNESIAN LEAGUE), WHICH IT DOMINATED. THROUGH THE LEAGUE AND BY DIRECT METHODS SPARTA WAS MASTER OF MOST OF THE PELOPONNESUS.

165

THE SPARTANS' WAY OF LIFE WOULD NOT HAVE BEEN POSSIBLE WITHOUT THEIR SLAVES, THE HELOTS, WHO HANDLED ALL THE DAILY TASKS AND UNSKILLED LABOR REQUIRED IN ORDER TO KEEP SPARTAN SOCIETY FUNCTIONING: THEY WERE THE FARMERS, DOMESTIC SERVANTS, NURSES AND MILITARY ATTENDANTS.

166

DESPITE THEIR MILITARY STRENGTH, THE SPARTANS' DOMINANCE WAS EVENTUALLY PUT TO AN ABRUPT END:

IN 371 B.C., THE SPARTANS WERE SUFFERED A CRUSHING DEFEAT AT THE HANDS OF THEBES AT THE BATTLE OF LEUCTRA,

THE SPARTAN EMPIRE THEN WENT INTO A SHARP DECLINE.

167

THE SPARTANS SUFFERED A HORRENDOUS DEFEAT AT THE HANDS OF EPAMINONDAS OF THEBES. A GREAT GENERAL AND STRATEGIST, EPAMINONDAS USED AN OBLIQUE FORMATION FOR HIS FORMATION, AND INCREASED THE DEPTH OF HIS MEN OPPOSITE THE SPARTANS FROM THE USUAL 8-12 TO 50 MEN DEEP, ALLOWING HIM TO OVERRUN THE SPARTAN POSITION.

168

THE SPARTAN'S PRIMARY WEAPON WAS CALLED A DORU. THE DORU WAS A 7-9 FOOT LONG SPEAR AND IT HAD A LEAF SHAPED HEAD, WITH A BRONZE SPIKE ON THE OTHER END. THIS SPIKE COULD BE USED TO FINISH OFF ENEMY DYING, OR IF NEED BE A REPLACEMENT SPEARHEAD IF THE TIP BROKE OFF.

169

BEFORE BATTLE, SPARTANS WOULD OFTEN TELL STORIES OF MARTIAL VALOR AND COURAGE TO INSPIRE TROOPS AND SANG MANLY SONGS TO CALM THEIR NERVES.

170

THE SPARTANS CONTINUED USING THE TRADITIONAL HOPLITE PHALANX UNTIL THE REFORMS OF KING CLEOMENES III, THE REFORMS RE-EQUIPPED THE SPARTAN ARMY WITH THE MACEDONIAN SARISSA (PIKE) AND TRAINED IN THE STYLE OF THE MACEDONIAN PHALANX.

171

THE SPARTAN KINGS AGIS IV (244-241 B.C.), FOLLOWED BY CLEOMENES III (235-221 B.C.), IN AN ATTEMPT TO RESTORE SPARTA MILITARY MIGHT, USHERED IN REFORMS THAT CLEARED DEBT, RE-DISTRIBUTED LAND, AND ALLOWED NON-CITIZENS TO BECOME SPARTANS. THIS EXPANDED THE CITIZEN BODY TO AROUND 4,000. THOUGH THE REFORMS SAW SOME SUCCESS, CLEOMENES III WAS ULTIMATELY FORCED TO YIELD THE CITY TO ACHAEAN LEAGUE CONTROL.

172

ONE SPARTAN, BEING ASKED A QUESTION, ANSWERED "NO." AND WHEN THE QUESTIONER SAID, "YOU LIE," THE OTHER SAID, "YOU SEE, THEN, THAT IT IS SILLY OF YOU TO ASK QUESTIONS TO WHICH YOU KNOW THE ANSWER!"

173

A SPARTAN, UPON BEING ASKED WHAT KIND OF A MAN TYRTAEUS THE POET WAS,

SAID:

"A GOOD MAN TO SHARPEN THE SPIRIT OF YOUTH."

174

A SPARTAN BOY, BEING TAKEN CAPTIVE BY ANTIGONUS THE KING AND SOLD, WAS OBEDIENT IN ALL ELSE TO THE ONE WHO HAD BOUGHT HIM, THAT IS, IN EVERYTHING WHICH HE THOUGHT FITTING FOR A FREE PERSON TO DO, BUT WHEN HIS OWNER BADE HIM BRING HIM A CHAMBER-POT, HE WOULD NOT BROOK SUCH TREATMENT, SAYING, "I WILL NOT BE A SLAVE"; AND WHEN THE OTHER WAS INSISTENT, HE WENT UP TO THE ROOF, AND SAYING, "YOU WILL GAIN MUCH BY YOUR

BARGAIN," HE THREW HIMSELF DOWN AND ENDED HIS LIFE

175

IN ANSWER TO THE THEBANS WHO WERE DISPUTING WITH THEM OVER SOME MATTERS, THEY SAID, "YOU SHOULD HAVE LESS PRIDE OR MORE POWER."

176

THE PERSIAN WARS WAS A MASSIVE CONFLICT THAT LASTED OVER FIFTY YEARS. SET BETWEEN THE ANCIENT EMPIRE OF PERSIA AND THE GREEK CITY STATES. THE BATTLE THAT BROUGHT IMMENSE FAME TO SPARTA WAS THE BATTLE OF THERMOPYLAE WHERE THE SPARTAN KING LEONIDAS, WITH ONLY THREE HUNDRED SPARTANS AND A FEW THOUSAND GREEKS, HELD OFF THE ENTIRE PERSIAN ARMY AT THE PASS OF THERMOPYLAE FOR MANY DAYS, UNTIL THE SPARTANS AND THEIR ALLIES

WERE EVENTUALLY DEFEATED. THE TALES OF COURAGE OF THE HEROES AT THERMOPYLAE WOULD SPREAD LIKE WILDFIRE THROUGHTOUT GREECE, CAUSING THE ENTIRE COUNTRY TO UNIFY AGAINST THE INVADERS.

177

AFTER THE PERSIAN WARS TENSION WITH ATHENS ROSE, AND ATHENS GREW STRONGER. AN EARTHQUAKE AT SPARTA (464 BC), FOLLOWED BY A MESSENIAN REVOLT, GREATLY WEAKENED THE SPARTAN STATE. IN THE END, A DISPUTE WITH ATHENS CAME INDIRECTLY, PROVOKED BY CORINTHIAN FEARS OF ATHENIAN EXPANSION AND IMPERIALISM. THIS WAS THE GREAT PELOPONNESIAN WAR (431–404 BC), WHICH SAW THE DISMANTLEMENT OF THE ATHENIAN EMPIRE.

178

A SPARTAN, SEEING A MAN OFFERING UP A COLLECTION OF WEALTH FOR THE GODS, SAID THAT HE DID NOT THINK MUCH OF GODS WHO WERE POORER THAN HIMSELF.

179

ONE MAN WHO CAME TO SPARTA, AND OBSERVED THE HONOUR WHICH THE YOUNG RENDER TO THE OLD, SAID,

"ONLY IN SPARTA DOES IT PAY TO GROW OLD."

180

KRYPTEIA

THE KRYPTEIA WAS COMPOSED OF HANDPICKED SPARTAN YOUTHS WHO DEMONSTRATED HIGH PROMISE AND EMBODIED ALL SPARTAN VIRTUES. THE KRYPTEIA ACTED AS A SORT OF POLICE FORCE/SPY NETWORK/ASSASSIN NETWORK. THE YOUTHS WOULD PATROL SPARTAN LAND AT NIGHT MAINTAIN SECURITY, GATHERING INTELLIGENCE AND PROTECTING AGAINST ROBBING GANGS. THEY LIVED IN THE WILD, ARMED ONLY WITH A KNIFE, AND WOULD

OFTEN KILL REBELLIOUS HELOTS AS A WAY TO KEEP THE SLAVE CASTE IN CHECK. THE KRYPTEIA WERE HIGH FEARED BY ALL.

181

THE GREEK LETTER LAMBDA (Λ), STOOD FOR LACONIA OR LACEDAEMON. THE SYMBOL WAS FIRST ADOPTED AROUND 400 B.C AND BECOME WIDELY KNOWN AS THE SYMBOL PAINTED ON SPARTAN SHIELDS.

182

IT WAS CUSTOM FOR SPARTAN FAMILIES TO PASS DOWN SHIELDS AS HEIRLOOMS FOR FUTURE GENERATIONS.

183

IT WAS NOT UNUSUAL FOR SPARTAN SURVIVORS WHO WERE DEFEATED IN BATTLE TO BE MOCKED AND HARASSED MERCILESSLY UPON RETURN FROM SPARTA. SEEN AS COWARDS AND TRAITORS FOR NOT FALLING IN BATTLE BESIDE THEIR BRETHREN, MANY WOULD TAKE THEIR OWN LIFE OUT OF SHAME OR EXILE THEMSELVES FROM SPARTA.

184

IF A SPARTAN CRIED OUT WHILE YOU WERE FIGHTING THEN NOT ONLY WERE YOU PUNISHED BUT YOUR BEST FRIEND/MENTOR WAS PUNISHED AS WELL.

185

OLDER BOYS HAD YOUNGER BOYS TO SERVE THEM. IF THE YOUNGER BOY DID SOMETHING WRONG THEN A COMMON PUNISHMENT WAS A BITE ON THE BACK OF THE HAND.

186

"YOU SEE, FELLOW CITIZENS. THAT THESE DOGS BELONG TO THE SAME STOCK. THOUGH BY VIRTUE OF DISCIPLINE TO WHICH THEY HAVE BEEN SUBJECTED THEY HAVE TURNED OUT UTTERLY DIFFERENT FROM EACH OTHER."

"SEE THEN, THAT TRAINING IS MORE EFFECTIVE THAN NATURE FOR THE GOOD OF MAN."

187

LYCURGUS IS SAID TO BE THE LAWGIVER AND FOUNDER OF THE ADMIRABLE VIRTUES DISPLAYED BY SPARTAN CITIZENS: MILITARY FITNESS, AUSTERITY, AND EQUALITY. HE IS SAID TO HAVE BEEN AN EXTREMELY HARD WORKER AND A COMPLETELY SOBER MAN. OFTEN CITED AS BEING GENTLE, FORGIVING, AND NEVER LOSING HIS TEMPER IN ANY SITUATION, HE WAS THE EMBODIMENT OF THE IDEAL SPARTAN CITIZEN.

188

TO TOUGHEN YOUNG SPARTANS AND ENCOURAGE THEIR DEVELOPMENT AS DISCIPLINED SOLDIERS, INSTRUCTORS WOULD OFTEN INSTIGATE FIGHTS BETWEEN TRAINEES

189

"WHAT A GOOD THING IT IS, FRIENDS. TO SHOW IN ACTUAL PRACTICE THE TRUE CHARACTERISTIC OF WEALTH. THAT IT IS BLIND."

-LYCURGUS

190

THE SPARTANS WERE FAMOUS FOR THEIR PHYSICAL FITNESS AND ADHERENCE TO NUTRIENT RICH DIET. THEY RESERVED A SPECIAL HATRED FOR OVERWEIGHT CITIZENS, WHO WERE OFTEN PUBLICLY RIDICULED, HARASSED AND RISKED BEING BANISHED FROM SPARTA

191

IT IS SAID THE VERY MENTION OF A SPARTAN ARMY ON THE MARCH WAS ENOUGH FOR SOME GREEK CITIES TO SUE FOR PEACE, SO MIGHTY WAS THEIR REPUTATION.

192

"A CITY IS NOT UNFORTIFIED WHOSE CROWN JEWEL IS HER MEN AND NOT BRICK AND STONE."

-LYCRUGUS

193

"MANY LONG, DEADLY SPEARS THRUSTED TOWARDS THE PERSIAN NECKS. DECADES OF SPARTAN MILITARY TRAINING HAD ALREADY TAUGHT THEM THE WEAK SPOTS OF AN ENEMY'S EQUIPMENT. COMPARED TO GREEK ARMOUR, THE PERSIANS ARMOUR WAS VASTLY INFERIOR. ADVANCING AGAINST THE PHALANX A PERSIAN MIGHT HAVE A SHIELD AND HELMET MADE OF REEDS, WOOD AND CLOTH, FACING SHIELDS MADE OF BRONZE AND HARDENED WOOD. THE PERSIANS WEAPONS OF

CHOICE INCLUDED A SPEAR AND A SHORT SWORD, ADVANCING EITHER AT A RUN OR IN NO PARTICULAR ORDER OR COHESION."

-BATTLE OF THERMOPYLAE

194

PAUSANIAS WAS THE NEPHEW OF KING LEONIDAS. AFTER HIS UNCLE'S DEATH, PAUSANIAS WENT ON TO DRIVE THE LAST OF THE PERSIAN ARMIES FROM GREECE. HE THEN WOULD TRY TO EXPAND SPARTA'S BORDERS BY WORKING WITH FOREIGN POWERS. HE WAS EXECUTED FOR TREASON AGAINST SPARTA.

195

AROUND 650 BC, THE MESSENIANS, LED BY ARISTOMENES, REVOLTED AGAINST THE SPARTANS. IT WOULD TAKE THE SPARTA TWENTY HARD FOUGHT YEARS TO SUBDUE THE REBELLION.

196

OF ALL THE NUMEROUS LAND BATTLES BETWEEN SPARTA AND ATHENS DURING THE PELOPONNESIAN WAR, SPARTA WOULD CLAIM VICTORY AT ALL BUT TWO, THE BATTLE OF CYTHERA AND THE BATTLE OF PYLOS.

197

"THE ATHENIANS WERE ONCE AGAIN FORCED TO TAKE REFUGE BEHIND THEIR MIGHTY WALLS, YET WITH LITTLE SUPPLIES, THEY WOULD EVENTUALLY SURRENDER TO SPARTA IN 404 B.C. RESULTING IN THE END OF THE PELOPONNESIAN WAR.

THUS USHERING IN THE TIME OF SPARTA'S DOMINANCE AND POLITICAL INFLUENCE IN GREECE AND THE END OF THE ONCE GREAT "ATHENIAN EMPIRE"

198

AROUND THE 6TH CENTURY B.C. THE SPARTANS BEGAN A "STYLE" THAT WOULD LAST FOR MANY YEARS. THE SPARTANS WOULD LET THEIR HAIR GROW LONG AND FLAUNT NO MOUSTACHES. ONLY AFTER A VICTORY WOULD THEY CUT THEIR HAIR AGAIN.

199

THE SPARTAN HEGEMONY AT ITS HEIGHT LASTED 33 YEARS BEFORE ITS DEFEAT AT LEUCTRA, AND IT WAS THE PROUDEST STATE IN GREECE.

200

KING AGESILAUS RULED SPARTA AT THE PINNACLE OF ITS POWER. HE CAMPAIGNED AGAINST PERSIA AND WAS NEVER DEFEATED. HE WOULD PROVE A UNIFIED GREECE WAS CAPABLE OF TAKING THE OFFENSIVE TO THE PERSIAN EMPIRE. THOUGH SUCCESSFUL, HE WAS CALLED BACK TO SPARTA DUE TO TROUBLE IN GREECE.

ALEXANDER (THE GREAT) OF MACEDON WOULD FOLLOW IN HIS FOOTSTEPS AND GO ON TO TOPPLE THE ENTIRE PERSIAN EMPIRE

201

"AFTER A DAY OF BATTLE, THE CALL FINALLY CAME FOR THE PERSIANS TO RETREAT, FINDING THAT DESPITE ALL THEIR EFFORT, THEY COULD NOT TAKE THE PASS FROM THE GREEKS. WHETHER ATTACKING IN WAVES OR IN FULL FORCE, IT CAME TO NO AVAIL THE PERSIANS RETURNED TO THEIR CAMPS FOR THE DAY."

-BATTLE OF THERMOPYLAE

202

"AROUND THE KING'S BODY, THE FIERCEST BATTLE TOOK PLACE. FOUR TIMES THE PERSIANS ATTACKED TO CLAIM HIS BODY AND FOUR TIMES THE KING'S MEN DENIED THEM."

-THERMOPYLAE, THE DEATH OF LEONIDAS

203

"THE SPARTANS FOUGHT ON TO THE LAST, SUCH THAT THOSE THAT STILL HAD SWORDS FOUGHT VICIOUSLY, WHILST THE OTHERS THREW ROCKS AND USED THEIR HANDS AND TEETH."

-BATTLE OF THERMOPYLAE

204

SPARTA'S ELECTIONS WERE ESSENTIALLY A MAJORITY RULED SHOUTING CONTEST. EVERY MALE CITIZEN OVER THE AGE OF THIRTY COULD PARTICIPATE. THIS SYSTEM OF VOTING WAS ADOPTED TO PREVENT ANY BIAS VOTING OR BRIBING THAT WAS COMMON IN EARLIER DEMOCRATIC ELECTIONS.

205

THE ICONIC CREST ATOP A SPARTAN HELMET WAS THOUGHT TO HAVE MADE A WARRIOR MORE FRIGHTENING BY GIVING HIM MORE HEIGHT.

206

A WARRIOR, IN THE THICK OF THE FIGHT, WAS ABOUT TO BRING DOWN HIS SWORD ON AN ENEMY WHEN THE RECALL SOUNDED, AND HE CHECKED THE BLOW. WHEN SOMEONE INQUIRED WHY, WHEN HE HAD HIS ENEMY IN HIS POWER, HE DID NOT KILL HIM, HE SAID, "BECAUSE IT IS BETTER TO OBEY ONE'S COMMANDER THAN TO SLAY AN ENEMY."

207

A BEGGAR ASKED OF A SPARTAN, WHO SAID, "IF I SHOULD GIVE TO YOU, YOU WILL BE THE MORE A BEGGAR; AND FOR THIS UNSEEMLY CONDUCT OF YOURS HE WHO FIRST GAVE YOU IS RESPONSIBLE, FOR HE THUS MADE YOU LAZY."

208

A SPARTAN, BEING ASKED WHY HE WORE HIS BEARD SO VERY LONG, SAID, "SO THAT I MAY SEE MY GREY HAIRS AND DO NOTHING UNWORTHY OF THEM."

209

AFTER THEIR SURRENDER, ATHENS WAS STRIPPED OF ITS MIGHTY WALLS, ITS FLEET AND ALL OF ITS OVERSEAS TERRITORY. THE CITY-STATES OF CORINTH AND THEBES CALLED FOR THE ENTIRE CITY OF ATHENS TO BE RAZED AND ALL HER CITIZENS EXECUTED OR ENSLAVED SPARTA REFUSED THEIR DEMANDS. THEY BELIEVED ATHENS HAD DONE GREAT SERVICE TO GREECE IN ITS TIME OF NEED. ATHENS, WHICH WAS AT ITS HEIGHT AND WAS CONSIDERED THE STRONGEST

CITY-STATE IN ALL OF GREECE BEFORE THE PELOPONNESIAN WAR, WAS DEVASTATED AND WOULD NEVER AGAIN REACH ITS PRE-WAR PROSPERITY. IN TURN, SPARTA BECAME THE LEADING GREEK CITY.

210

WHEN INVITED BY ALEXANDER THE GREAT TO JOIN HIS CAMPAGIN AGAINST THE PERSIANS, THE SPARTANS REFUSED.

THEY REPLIED TO ALEXANDER:

"THE SPARTANS DO NOT FOLLOW MEN, BUT LEAD THEM."

211

A SPARTAN'S SHIELD IS CALLED AN ASPIS. THE BULK OF THE SHIELD WAS THAT OF OAK AND WAS COVERED BY A THINNER LAYER OF BRONZE.

THE TOTAL WIDTH OF THE SHIELD WAS THREE FEET AND WOULD PROTECT ITS BEARER'S WHOLE BODY AND A THIRD OF THE MAN'S TO HIS RIGHT.

212

THE FULL HOPLITE EQUIPMENT WAS TERMED A **PANOPLIA**.

213

THE SPARTAN HOPLITE'S CAPE WAS RED SO THE ENEMY COULD NOT SEE THEIR BLOOD IF WOUNDED.

214

AFTER HAVING REJECTED THE GREAT KING'S OFFER FOR THE SPARTANS TO JOIN HIM ON HIS CAMPAIGN AGAINST THE PERSIAN EMPIRE, ALEXANDER THE GREAT SENT BACK TO GREECE HUNDREDS OF FALLEN PERSIANS OFFICER'S ARMOR AS TROPHIES OF WAR. STILL BITTER ABOUT THE SPARTANS REPLY, HE ATTACHED A MESSAGE TO THE TROPHIES WHICH READ:

"ALEXANDER, SON OF PHILIP, AND ALL THE GREEKS, EXCLUDING THE SPARTANS, GIVE THESE TROPHIES OF CONQUEST

TAKEN FROM THE BARBARIANS
OF ASIA."

215

SPARTAN BOYS ENROLLED IN ONE OF THE MANY TROOPS (THE AGELES), WHICH WAS UNDER THE SUPERVISION OF A SENIOR SPARTAN AND AT THIRTEEN UNDER THE LEADERSHIP OF A PRUDENT AND BRAVE YOUTH, CALLED EIRENA ,SUPERVISED BY AN OFFICIAL (PAIDONOMOS) AND WERE DRILLED IN GYMNASTICS, RUNNING, JUMPING, THROWING OF SPEAR AND DISCUS, AND ALSO TAUGHT TO ENDURE PAIN AND HARDSHIP, HUNGER, THIRST, COLD, FATIGUE AND LACK OF SLEEP.THEY WERE WALKING

WITHOUT SHOES, BATHED AT THE COLD WATERS OF THE RIVER EUROTAS AND WERE DRESSED WINTER AND SUMMER, WITH THE SAME PIECE OF CLOTH, WHICH THE STATE GAVE THEM ONCE A YEAR.

216

AS SOON AS A CHILD WAS BORN IN SPARTA, THE MOTHER WOULD WASH IT WITH WINE, IN ORDER TO MAKE SURE THAT IT WAS STRONG.

217

A MAN HAD TO REMAIN IN HIS BARRACKS UNTIL HE WAS 30 AND IF HE MARRIED (COULD MARRY FROM THE AGE OF 20) HE HAD TO VISIT HIS WIFE IN SECRECY.

218

ARCHIDAMUS, WHEN THE GREEKS WERE NOT WILLING TO TAKE HIS ADVICE AND BREAK THEIR AGREEMENTS WITH ANTIPATER AND CRATERUS THE MACEDONIAN, BAND BE FREE, BECAUSE OF A FEELING THAT THE SPARTANS WOULD BE HARSHER THAN THE MACEDONIANS, HE SAID, "A SHEEP OR A GOAT BLEATS ALWAYS IN THE SAME WAY, BUT A MAN TALKS IN A GREAT VARIETY OF WAYS UNTIL HE ACCOMPLISHES WHAT HE HAS SET HIS MIND UPON."

219

DEMETRIUS I OF MACEDON, WHEN THE SPARTANS SENT TO HIS COURT A SINGLE ENVOY, WAS OFFENDED AND EXCLAIMED ANGRILY, "WHAT! HAVE THE LACEDAEMONIANS SENT NO MORE THAN ONE AMBASSADOR?"

THE SPARTAN RESPONDED,

"AYE, ONE AMBASSADOR TO ONE KING."

220

At the time when Thebans had conquered the Spartans at Leuctra and advanced to the river Eurotas itself, one of them, boasting, said, "Where are the Spartans now?" A Spartan who had been captured by them said, "They are not here; otherwise you would not have come thus far."

221

A MAN WHO WAS VISITING SPARTA STOOD FOR A LONG TIME UPON ONE FOOT, AND SAID TO A SPARTAN, "I DO NOT THINK THAT YOU, SIR, COULD STAND UPON ONE FOOT AS LONG AS THAT"; AND THE OTHER INTERRUPTING SAID, "NO, BUT THERE IS NOT A SINGLE GOOSE THAT COULD NOT DO IT."

222

THE CRYPTEIA CONTROLLED THE SPARTAN'S SLAVES, THE HELOTS, USING A VARIETY OF METHODS FROM SIMPLE FEAR TO OUTRIGHT MURDER. THE ORGANIZATION USED THE NIGHT AS A CLOAK FOR ITS ACTIVITIES WHICH HELPED SPREAD FEAR AND EVEN TERROR. THE AVERAGE AGE OF A MEMBER WAS 18.

223

MEN TENDED TO MARRY IN THEIR PRIME, AND INTERESTINGLY, WHEN THEY GOT OLDER THEY WERE ENCOURAGED TO GIVE THEIR WIVES TO YOUNGER AND STRONGER MEN, SO THAT SHE WOULD CONTINUE TO PRODUCE STRONG CHILDREN. WOMEN WERE ALSO ENTITLED TO NEGOTIATE WITH THEIR HUSBANDS IF THEY WANTED TO TAKE A LOVER. SUCH ARRANGEMENTS WERE REASON FOR PRIDE, NOT SHAME, AS THE HUSBAND USUALLY CLAIMED THE CHILDREN AS HIS OWN.

224

. THE SPARTANS REFER TO THEMSELVES AS LACEDAEMONIANS. AFTER LACONIA, THE REGION OF GREECE WHERE SPARTA WAS LOCATED

225

THE GEROUSIA WAS A COUNCIL MADE UP OF 28 SPARTIATES (PLUS THE TWO KINGS), WHO ACTED IN AN ADVISORY CAPACITY, AS WELL AS PRESIDING AT CRIMINAL TRIALS. TO BE APPOINTED TO THE GEROUSIA, YOU HAD TO BE AT LEAST 60 YEARS OLD, AND BE A PARTICULARLY VIRTUOUS PERSON ALL ROUND.

226

THE SPARTANS WERE THE ONLY SOLDIERS IN GREECE TO WEAR A MILITARY UNIFORM. THEY ALL DONNED THE SAME ARMOR AND SHIELD.

227

THERE WERE NEVER MORE THAN 10,000 SPARTIATES AT ANYTIME.

228

DURING THE AGOGE, BOYS WERE ENCOURAGED TO SCAVENGE AND STEAL FOR THEIR FOOD. IF CAUGHT HOWEVER THEY WERE PUNISHED - NOT FOR THE THEFT - BUT FOR BEING CAUGHT DOING IT.

229

SHORTLY AFTER BIRTH, A SPARTAN BABY WOULD BE PRESENTED TO AN ELDER SPARTAN. IF ANY WEAKNESS OR DEFORMITY WAS DISCOVERED, THE BABY WOULD BE THROWN OFF MOUNT TAYGETOS AND LEFT TO DIE.

230

In answer to the Argives, who were disputing with the Spartans in regard to the boundaries of their land and said that they had the better of the case, p375he drew his sword and said, "He who is master of this talks best about boundaries of land."

231

HERONDAS WAS AT ATHENS WHEN A MAN THERE WAS FOUND GUILTY ON A CHARGE OF NOT HAVING ANY OCCUPATION, AND WHEN HE HEARD OF THIS, HE BADE THEM POINT OUT TO HIM THE MAN WHO HAD BEEN CONVICTED OF THE FREEMAN'S CRIME!

232

A SPARTAN TAKEN CAPTIVE WAS BEING SOLD, WHEN SOMEONE SAID, "IF I BUY YOU, WILL YOU BE GOOD AND HELPFUL?" SAID, "YES, IF YOU DO NOT BUY ME."

233

AFTER THE SPARTAN DEFEAT OF AGIS, ANTIPATER DEMANDED FIFTY BOYS AS HOSTAGES, BUT ETEOCLES, WHO WAS EPHOR, SAID THEY WOULD NOT GIVE BOYS, LEST THE BOYS SHOULD TURN OUT TO BE UNEDUCATED THROUGH MISSING THE TRADITIONAL DISCIPLINE; AND THEY WOULD NOT BE FITTED FOR CITIZENSHIP EITHER. BUT THE SPARTANS WOULD GIVE, IF HE SO DESIRED, EITHER OLD MEN OR WOMEN TO DOUBLE THE NUMBER. WHEN ANTIPATER MADE DIRE THREATS IF HE

SHOULD NOT GET THE BOYS, THE SPARTANS MADE ANSWER WITH ONE CONSENT, "IF THE ORDERS YOU LAY UPON US ARE HARSHER THAN DEATH, WE SHALL FIND IT EASIER TO DIE."

234

SPARTAN MILTARY PRESTIGE WAS DEALT A SEVERE BLOW WHEN A UNIT OF 600 MEN WAS DECIMATED BY ATHENIAN PELTASTS.

235

SPARTANS DID NOT TYPICALLY MAKE USE OF CAVALRY. IT WAS NOT UNTIL THE LATER YEARS OF THE PELOPONNESIAN WAR THAT SPARTAN ARMIES WOULD HAVE SMALL UNITS OF CAVALRY ATTACHED.

236

AT THE TIME WHEN THE ATHENIANS HAD SURRENDERED THEIR CITY, THEY DECLARED IT WAS ONLY RIGHT THAT SAMOS SHOULD BE LEFT TO THEM, BUT THE SPARTANS SAID, "DO YOU, AT A TIME WHEN YOU DO NOT EVEN OWN YOURSELVES, SEEK TO POSSESS OTHERS?" FROM THIS INCIDENT AROSE THE PROVERB:

237

SPARTAN MEN HAD LONG, DREADLOCKED HAIR, WHICH THEY BELIEVED MADE THEM MORE TERRIFYING AND APPEAR MORE DIGNIFIED.

238

THE SPARTANS WERE KNOWN TO HAVE PRACTICED PYRRICHE.

PYRRICHE IS A DANCE IN WHICH THE DANCER WOULD CARRY WEAPONS IN ORDER TO TRAIN HIS MOVEMENTS UNDER ARMS TO EVADE ENEMY ATTACKS WHILST DELIVERING HIS OWN KILLING BLOWS.

239

THE EPHORS WERE A BRANCH OF SPARTAN GOVERNMENT WITH NO EQUIVALENT IN THE REST OF THE GREEK WORLD. THEY WERE ELECTED ANNUALLY FROM THE POOL OF MALE CITIZENS. THEIR ROLE WAS TO BALANCE AND COMPLEMENT THE ROLE OF THE KING. THEY WERE THE SUPREME CIVIL COURT AND HAD CRIMINAL JURISDICTION OVER THE KING.

240

THE BOYS WERE FIGHTING, AND ONE OF THEM WOUNDED THE OTHER MORTALLY WITH THE STROKE OF A SICKLE. THE FRIENDS OF THE WOUNDED BOY, AS THEY WERE ABOUT TO SEPARATE, PROMISED TO AVENGE HIM AND MAKE AWAY WITH THE ONE WHO HAD STRUCK HIM, BUT THE BOY SAID, "IN HEAVEN'S NAME DO NOT, FOR IT IS NOT RIGHT; THE FACT IS, I SHOULD HAVE DONE THAT MYSELF IF I HAD BEEN QUICK ENOUGH AND BRAVE ENOUGH."

241

WHEN TWO MEN WERE PUBLICLY SHAMED FOR NOT BEING PART OF THE "HEROIC" BATTLE OF THERMOPYLAE, THE FIRST MAN HUNG HIMSELF, WHILE THE SECOND REDEEMED HIMSELF BY BEING KILLED IN A LATER BATTLE.

242

"BEFORE YOU CROSS THE BORDER OF DEATH, YOU SHOULD REACH THE LIMITS OF VIRTUE"

-TYRTAEUS OF SPARTA

243

LACONOPHILIA IS LOVE OR ADMIRATION OF SPARTA AND OF THE SPARTAN CULTURE OR CONSTITUTION.

244

AFTER THE DISASTTROUS BATTLE OF LEUCTRA, THE THEBANS LIBERATED THE MESSENIANS FROM SPARTAN RULE. MESSENE BECAME AN INDEPENDENT CITY-STATE ONCE AGAIN. WITHOUT THEIR FORCE LABOR, THE SPARTANS COULD NOT MAINTAIN ITS ICON MILITARY WAY OF LIFE AND FELL INTO A JUST ANOTHER MINOR GREEK CITY-STATE.

245

A LAME MAN WAS GOING FORTH TO WAR, AND SOME PERSONS FOLLOWED AFTER HIM LAUGHING. HE TURNED AROUND AND SAID, "YOU VILE FOOLS! A MAN DOES NOT NEED TO RUN AWAY WHEN HE FIGHTS THE ENEMY, BUT TO STAY WHERE HE IS AND HOLD HIS GROUND."

246

WHEN ASKED WHY HE WORE HIS HAIR AND BEARD LONG, A SPARTAN REPLIED:

"SO I MAY SEE MY GREY HAIRS AND NEVER DO ANYTHING UNWORTHY OF THEM."

247

HIPPODAMUS, WHEN AGIS WAS TAKING HIS PLACE ON THE FIELD OF BATTLE BESIDE ARCHIDAMUS, WAS SENT WITH AGIS TO SPARTA TO RENDER HIS SERVICES THERE. "BUT LOOK YOU," SAID HE, "I SHALL MEET NO MORE HONOURABLE DEATH THAN IN PLAYING THE PART OF A BRAVE MAN FOR SPARTA'S SAKE." (HE WAS OVER EIGHTY YEARS OLD.) AND THEREUPON, SEIZING HIS ARMS AND TAKING HIS STAND AT THE KING'S RIGHT HAND, HE FELL FIGHTING.

248

When Philip invaded the Peloponnesus, and someone said, "There is danger that the Spartans may meet a dire fate if they do not make terms with the invader," Damindas exclaimed, "You poor womanish thing! What dire fate could be ours if we have no fear of death?"

249

WHEN SOMEONE, WISHING TO INTRODUCE A MUSICIAN TO HIM, SAID, IN ADDITION TO OTHER COMMENDATIONS, THAT THE MAN WAS THE BEST MUSICIAN AMONG THE GREEKS, CLEOMENES POINTED TO ONE OF THE PERSONS NEAR, AND SAID, "YONDER MAN, I SWEAR, RANKS WITH ME AS THE BEST SOUP-MAKER."

250

KING DEMARATUS, ANNOYED WITH A MAN CONSTANTLY ASKING WHO THE PERFECT SPARTAN WAS,

FINALLY REPLIED:

"THE ONE WHO IS LEAST LIKE YOU!"

251

WHEN AN ARGIVE SAID ONCE UPON A TIME, "THERE ARE MANY TOMBS OF SPARTANS IN OUR COUNTRY," A SPARTAN SAID, "BUT THERE IS NOT A SINGLE TOMB OF AN ARGIVE IN OUR COUNTRY," INDICATING BY THIS THAT THE SPARTANS HAD OFTEN SET FOOT IN ARGOS, BUT THE ARGIVES HAD NEVER SET FOOT IN SPARTA·

252

SOMEONE REMARKED THAT THE ENEMIES NUMBERS WERE SUBSTANTIAL. THE SPARTAN COMMANDER SAID, "THEN WE WILL WIN GREATER FAME SINCE WE WILL INFLICT HIGHER CASUALTIES."

253

"AN HONORABLE DEATH IS PREFERABLE TO A DISHONORABLE LIFE.... AT LACEDAEMON EVERYONE WOULD BE ASHAMED TO ALLOW A COWARD INTO THE SAME TENT AS HIMSELF, OR ALLOW HIM TO BE HIS OPPONENT IN A MATCH AT WRESTLING...."

254

THE CITY-STATE OF ARGOS, NOT ATHENS, IS CONSIDERED TO BE THE TRUE RIVAL OF SPARTA. THROUGHOUT THEIR HISTORY, THE TWO CITIES WERE CONSTANTLY AT WAR WITH ONE ANOTHER.

255

IN THE YEAR 421 BC A PEACE TREATY WAS SIGNED BETWEEN THE SPARTA AND ATHENS KNOWN AS THE "PEACE OF NICIAS", WHICH WAS SUPPOSED TO LAST 50 YEARS. IT LASTED SEVEN.

256

IN 394 B.C, AT THE BATTLE OF NEMEA, A FORCE OF UNIFIED THEBAN, ATHENIAN, AND ARGIVES MARCHED ON A MUCH SMALLER SPARTAN ARMY. DESPITE BEING OUTNUMBERED, THE SPARTANS CRUSHED THE GREEK COALILITION.

257

"THE KING DIVIDED HIS HOPLITES INTO SIX MORAI [REGIMENTS] OF CAVALRY AND HEAVY INFANTRY. EACH OF THESE HOPLITE MORAI HAS ONE POLEMARCHOS [COLONEL], FOUR LOCHAGOI [CAPTAINS], EIGHT PENTECONTERS [LIEUTENANTS], AND SIXTEEN ENOMOTARCHS [SERGEANTS]. AT A WORD OF COMMAND ANY SUCH MORAI CAN BE FORMED READILY INTO EITHER ENOMOTIES [SINGLE-FILE], OR INTO THREES [THREE FILES OF MEN ABREAST] OR SIXES [SIX FILES OF MEN ABREAST]."

-XENOPHON, THE SPARTAN WAR MACHINE

258

THE YOUNGER AGIS, WHEN DEMADES SAID THAT THE JUGGLERS WHO SWALLOW SWORDS USE THE SPARTAN SWORDS BECAUSE OF THEIR SHORTNESS, RETORTED, "BUT ALL THE SAME THE SPARTANS REACH THEIR ENEMIES WITH THEIR SWORDS.

259

ANOTHER SPARTAN CAPTIVE BEING PUT UP FOR SALE, WHEN THE CRIER THAT HE WAS OFFERING A SLAVE FOR SALE, SAID, "YOU DAMNABLE WRETCH, WON'T YOU SAY 'A CAPTIVE'?"

260

TWO EPHORS WOULD ALWAYS ACCOMPANY THE KING. (ONLY ONE KING WENT TO WAR WHILE THE OTHER STAYED AT SPARTA) THE EPHORS WOULD SUPERVISE AND MONITOR THE KING; THEY COULD ALSO ISSUE ORDERS TO GENERALS AND DECIDE WHICH TROOPS WERE SENT TO WAR!

261

ANY SPARTA CITIZEN WHO WAS IN POOR FITNESS OR OVERWEIGHT RISKED BEING RIDICULED AND THROWN OUT OF THE CITY.

262

CLEOMENES, THE SON OF CLEOMBROTUS, WHEN SOMEONE OFFERED HIM FIGHTING COCKS AND SAID THAT THEY WOULD DIE FIGHTING FOR VICTORY, SAID, "WELL THEN, GIVE ME SOME OF THOSE THAT KILL THEM, FOR THOSE ARE BETTER THAN THESE.

263

PLEISTARCHUS, WHEN SOMEONE SAID THAT A CERTAIN EVIL-SPEAKER WAS COMMENDING HIM, HE SAID, "I WONDER WHETHER POSSIBLY SOMEONE MAY NOT HAVE TOLD HIM THAT I WAS DEAD; FOR THE MAN CAN NEVER SAY A GOOD WORD OF ANYBODY WHO IS ALIVE."

264

When someone, initiating a Spartan into the mysteries, asked him what his conscience told him was the most unholy deed he had ever done, he said, "The gods know." And when the other became even more insistent, and said, "It is absolutely necessary that you tell," the Spartan asked in turn, "To whom must I tell it? To you or the god?" And when the other said, "To the god," the Spartan said, "Then go away."

265

"SO THAT, BY FOLLOWING THE SAME PRACTICES AS THE MEN, MAY NOT BE INFERIOR TO THEM IN BODILY STRENGTH AND HEALTH OR IN MENTAL SHARPNESS AND ASPIRATIONS."

-LYCURGUS, ON SPARTAN WOMEN TRAINING AND SCHOOLING

266

KING DARIUS I, RULER OF THE PERSIAN EMPIRE, SENT ENVOYS TO SPARTA AND ATHENS. THE KING DEMANDED THAT THEY GIVE THE PERSIAN EMPIRE "EARTH AND WATER". THE SPARTANS, UPON HEARING THE DEMAND, THREW THE PERSIAN ENVOY DOWN A WELL, AFTER TELLING THE ENVOY HE WOULD FIND MUCH EARTH AND WATER DOWN THE WELL.

267

WHEN SOMEONE INQUIRED WHY THEY TOOK THEIR GIRLS INTO PUBLIC PLACES UNVEILED, BUT THEIR MARRIED WOMEN VEILED, CHARILLUS SAID, "BECAUSE THE GIRLS HAVE TO FIND HUSBANDS, AND THE MARRIED WOMEN HAVE TO KEEP TO THOSE WHO HAVE THEM!"

268

CLEOMENES OF SPARTA MARCHED HIS ARMY INTO ARGOLIS, BUT HE HAD FAILED TO TAKE THE CITY OF ARGOS ITSELF. THOUGH IN THAT SAME YEAR, HE AMBUSHED AND SCATTERED THE ARGIVE ARMY. THE SURVIVING ARGIVES ATTEMPTED TO TAKE REFUGE IN A HOLY GROVE DEDICATED TO THE MYTHICAL HERO ARGOS. CLEOMENES WITHOUT REMORSE, SET FIRE TO THE GROVE. THE HIDING ARGIVES WERE BURNED ALIVE OR DRIVEN OUT AND KILLED. IN THE END, THE ARGIVE CASUALTIES

NUMBERED NEAR 6,500, OVER TWO THIRDS THE ENTIRE ARGIVE ARMY.

269

THE SPARTANS, HAVING DEFEATED THE ARGIVE ARMY, WOULD MAKE SURE THE CITY OF ARGOS WOULD NEVER THREATEN ARROS AGAIN. THE SPARTANS SACKED THE CITY AND HAD ALL THE MALE CITIZENS EXECUTED.

270

WHEN THEIR KING PROMISED TO WIPE OUT COMPLETELY ANOTHER CITY WHICH, AS IT HAPPENED, HAD GIVEN MUCH TROUBLE TO THE SPARTANS, THEY WOULD NOT ALLOW IT, SAYING, "YOU MUST NOT ABOLISH NOR REMOVE THE WHETSTONE OF OUR YOUTH."

271

TEHOPOMPUS, WHEN THE PEOPLE OF PYLOS VOTED HIM SOME UNUSUALLY HIGH HONOURS, HE WROTE IN REPLY THAT TIME INCREASES MODEST HONOURS, BUT OBLITERATES THOSE THAT ARE EXTRAVAGANT.

272

WHEN SOMEONE SAID TO ASTYCRATIDAS, AFTER THE DEFEAT OF AGIS THEIR KING IN THE BATTLE AGAINST ANTIPATER IN THE VICINITY OF MEGALOPOLIS, "WHAT WILL YOU DO, MEN OF SPARTA? WILL YOU BE SUBJECT TO THE MACEDONIANS? HE SAID, "WHAT! IS THERE ANY WAY IN WHICH ANTIPATER CAN FORBID US TO DIE FIGHTING FOR SPARTA?"

273

"IN BATTLE, THE SPARTANS WOULD ADVANCE TOWARDS THE ENEMY TO IN TIME TO THE TUNE OF FLUTES. THIS WOULD ENSURE THAT THE PHALANX WOULD ADVANCE EVENLY AND AT THE SAME PACE. THIS GAVE THE SPARTANS A HUGE ADVANTAGE OVER OTHER ARMIES, AS IT WAS ORDINARY FOR LARGE ARMIES TO BREAK FORMATION AT THE MOMENT OF BATTLE.

274

WHEN PHILIP INVADED THE SPARTANS' LAND, AND ALL THOUGHT THAT THEY SHOULD BE DESTROYED, HE SAID TO ONE OF THE SPARTANS, "WHAT SHALL YOU DO NOW, MEN OF SPARTA?" THE SPARTAN SAID, "WHAT ELSE THAN DIE LIKE MEN? FOR WE ALONE OF ALL THE GREEKS HAVE LEARNED TO BE FREE, AND NOT TO BE SUBJECT TO OTHERS."

275

UPON BEING ASKED WHO WAS THE BEST SPARTIATE:

"THE ONE LEAST LKE YOU..."

276

"FURTHER, THE LAW ENJOINS UPON ALL SPARTANS, DURING THE WHOLE PERIOD OF THE CAMPAIGN, THE CONSTANT PRACTICE OF GYMNASTIC EXERCISES, WHEREBY THEIR PRIDE IN THEMSELVES IS INCREASED, AND THEY APPEAR FREER AND OF A MORE LIBERAL ASPECT THAN THE REST OF THE WORLD." -XENOPHON

277

WHEN SOME COMMENDED THE PEOPLE OF ELIS BECAUSE THEY WERE VERY JUST IN CONDUCTING THE OLYMPIC GAMES, KING AGIS SAID,

"WHAT GREAT OR MARVELLOUS ACCOMPLISHMENT IS IT IF THEY PRACTISE JUSTICE ON ONE DAY ONLY IN FOUR YEARS?"

278

ONCE UPON A TIME, AMBASSADORS FROM SPARTA ARRIVED AT THE COURT OF LYGDAMIS THE DESPOT. BUT AS HE TRIED TO PUT THEM OFF AND REPEATEDLY POSTPONED THE INTERVIEW, AND, TO CROWN ALL, IT WAS ASSERTED THAT HE WAS IN A DELICATE CONDITION, THE SPARTANS SAID, "TELL HIM, IN ZEUS'S NAME, THAT WE HAVE NOT COME TO WRESTLE WITH HIM, BUT TO HAVE A TALK WITH HIM."

279

When someone inquired why they kept the laws in regard to bravery unwritten, and did not have them written down and thus give them to the young men to read, Zeuxidamus said, "Because the young ought to accustom themselves to deeds of manly valour, a better thing than to apply their mind to writings."

280

ARCHIDAMUS, THE SON OF AGESILAUS, WHEN PHILIP, AFTER THE BATTLE OF CHAERONEIA, WROTE HIM A SOMEWHAT HAUGHTY LETTER, WROTE IN REPLY,

"IF YOU SHOULD MEASURE YOUR OWN SHADOW, YOU WOULD NOT FIND THAT IT HAS BECOME ANY GREATER THAN BEFORE YOU WERE VICTORIOUS."

281

CALLICRATIDAS, AS HE OFFERED SACRIFICE BEFORE THE BATTLE, AND HEARD FROM THE SEER THAT THE INDICATIONS OF THE OMENS WERE VICTORY FOR THE ARMY, BUT DEATH FOR ITS COMMANDER, HE SAID, NOT AT ALL DISCONCERTED, "SPARTA'S FATE RESTS NOT WITH ONE MAN. FOR, IF I AM KILLED, MY COUNTRY WILL NOT BE IMPAIRED IN ANY WAY; BUT IF I YIELD TO THE ENEMY, IT WILL BE." AND SO, AFTER APPOINTING CLEANDER TO TAKE HIS PLACE AS COMMANDER, HE PUT FORTH WITHOUT DELAY

FOR THE NAVAL ENGAGEMENT, AND MET HIS DEATH IN THE BATTLE.

282

THE EVENT THAT CAUSED THE MOST SURPRISE AMONGST THE GREEKS IN THE PELOPONESSIAN WAR WAS THE SURRENDER OF A SPARTAN FORCE AT SPHARCTERIA. UNTIL THEN IT WAS UNHEARD OF FOR ANY SPARTAN FORCE TO SURRENDER ON ANY TERMS.

283

In a clinch, one wrestler, who had the other by the neck, overpowered him with little effort, and pulled him to the ground. Since the one who was down was at a disadvantage in using his body, he bit the arm that held him. His opponent said, "Spartan, you bite like a woman." "No, indeed," said he, "but like a lion."

284

A SPARTAN BEING ASKED WHAT HE KNEW, SAID,

"HOW TO BE FREE"

285

THE SPARTANS, THOUGH ONLY A SHADOW OF THEIR FORMER MILITARY MIGHT, DEFEATED THE ARGIVE ARMY AND SACKED THE CITY OF ARGOS TWICE, BOTH IN 225 AND 196 BC.

286

SPARTA BECAME A WIDELY VISITED "TOURIST ATTRACTION" BY WEALTHY ROMANS, FASCINATED BY THE WARRIOR CULTURE AND SIMPLE WAY OF LIFE THE SPARTANS ENDURED.

287

SPARTA REMAINED AN INDEPENDENT CITY-STATE UNTIL 146 BC AFTER BEING DEFEATED AND ANNEXED BY ROME.

288

IT IS SAID THAT AFTER THE CRUSHING DEFEAT OF THE ROMAN ARMY AT THE BATTLE OF ADRIANOPLE IN 378 AD, A RAIDING FORCE OF GOTHS IN GREECE WERE MET BY A PHALANX OF SPARTAN MILITIA AND SOUNDLY DEFEATED.

289

THE ANCIENT CITY OF SPARTA WAS DESTROYED BY VISIGOTHS IN AD 396. THE MODERN TOWN, CALLED NEW SPARTA LOCALLY, WAS BUILT IN 1834 AFTER THE WAR OF GREEK INDEPENDENCE.

290

IN 1834, OTTO (1815-67), THE KING OF GREECE, ORDERED THE FOUNDING OF THE MODERN-DAY TOWN OF SPARTON, THE SITE OF ANCIENT SPARTA.

291

SPARTA WAS USED AS A MODEL OF SOCIAL PURITY BY REVOLUTIONARY AND NAPOLEONIC FRANCE

292

A NUMBER OF MILITARY AIRCRAFT HAVE NAMES DERIVED FROM THE SPARTANS.

SUCH AS THE C-27A SPARTAN AND THE ALENIA C-27J SPARTAN.

293

THE ICONIC HELMET OF THE SPARTAN HOPLITE WAS THE CORINTHIAN HELMET

294

SPARTAN MILITARY TACTICS ARE STILL STUDIED, AND IMPLEMENTED AT MODERN MILITARY ACADEMIES AROUND THE WORLD

295

THE TOMB OF KING LEONIDAS IS LOCATED IN MODERN DAY SPARTA

296

DURING THE GREEK MONARCHY, THE TITLE OF "DUKE OF SPARTA" WAS USED FOR THE GREEK CROWN PRINCE

297

"SPARTATHLON" TAKES PLACE EVERY SEPTEMBER SINCE 1983, AN ULTRAMARATHON STARTING IN ATHENS AND ENDING IN SPARTA AT THE TOMB OF LEONIDAS

298

MODERN SPARTA IS CONSIDERED THE MOST CONSERVATIVE CITY IN GREECE

299

MODERN SPARTA WAS ONE OF THE FEW CITIES THAT VOTED IN SUPPORT OF RETAINING THE GREEK MONARCHY IN 1974

300

UNTIL MODERN TIMES, THE SITE OF ANCIENT SPARTA WAS OCCUPIED BY A SMALL TOWN OF A FEW THOUSAND PEOPLE WHO LIVED AMONGST THE RUINS.

THE END

Made in the USA
Lexington, KY
12 September 2016